Abridged Grammars of the Languages of the Cuneiform Inscriptions: Containing I.--A Sumero-Akkadian Grammar, Ii.--An Assyro-Babylonian Grammar, Iii.--A Vannic Grammar, Iv.--A Medic Grammar, V.--An Old Persian Grammar

George Bertin

LANGUAGES OF THE CUNEIFORM INSCRIPTIONS.

ABRIDGED GRAMMARS

OF THE

LANGUAGES OF THE CUNEIFORM INSCRIPTIONS

CONTAINING

I.—A SUMERO-AKKADIAN GRAMMAR
II.—AN ASSYRO-BABYLONIAN GRAMMAR
III.—A VANNIC GRAMMAR
IV.—A MEDIC GRAMMAR
V.—AN OLD PERSIAN GRAMMAR

BY

GEORGE BERTIN, M.R.A.S.

LONDON
TRÜBNER & CO., LUDGATE HILL
1888

Ballantyne Press
BALLANTYNE, HANSON AND CO.
EDINBURGH AND LONDON

TO

A. H. SAYCE, M.A.,

DEPUTY PROFESSOR OF COMPARATIVE PHILOLOGY IN THE
UNIVERSITY OF OXFORD,

WHO HAS, BY HIS RESEARCHES, HIS TEACHING, AND HIS DISCOVERIES,
DONE SO MUCH TO ADVANCE OUR KNOWLEDGE OF THE
LANGUAGES OF THE CUNEIFORM INSCRIPTIONS,

THIS WORK IS

Dedicated

AS A SMALL TRIBUTE

BY

THE AUTHOR.

PREFACE.

IN the following grammars I have endeavoured to follow the plan laid down by the late Professor Palmer in the first volume of the series, which is a model of concision and lucidity. The great difficulty I had to contend with is the fact that these languages have been dead for many centuries, and the texts—except for Assyro-Babylonian—are still very limited. The task would have been impossible without the efforts and labours of the first pioneers in the field, Sir H. C. Rawlinson, Dr. Hincks, Norris, Dr. J. Oppert, Professor Sayce, Professor Schrader, &c., to all of whom I am largely indebted.

For the transcription I have adopted the principle that the inscriptions themselves must be our sole guide, and that, rejecting all theories, all words ought to be transcribed as they are actually written, whatever might have been the pronunciation, as this cannot be stated with certainty. I give these languages as they are found on the inscriptions. Theoricians may afterwards, if they like, discuss the question of what might have been the pronunciation of the people. All the forms—except stem-words, and, for Babylonian, the infinitives of *kal*—given as examples in the following pages, are actually found in the inscriptions.

It must not be forgotten that the object in view in these grammars—as with all those of dead languages—is to facilitate to the student the reading of the texts, and not to teach him how to speak. Particular attention has, however, been given to the Syntax, so often neglected in works of this kind.

The Sumero-Akkadian grammar is practically the first written for this language, as the attempt of F. Lenormant was made at a time when a correct analysis of it was impossible.

In the Assyro-Babylonian grammar I have adopted an entirely new point of view, which has the advantage of making clear what could not be rationally explained before.

The Vannic grammar is based on the works of Professor A. H. Sayce, though I believe I have improved certain parts.[1]

For the Medic I have followed my first master, Dr. Oppert, and I am also much indebted to Professor Sayce.

In the Old Persian studies all is due to Sir H. Rawlinson, Dr. Oppert, and Dr. Spiegel, and I follow them on the main points.

I must also acknowledge the help I have received from my friend Mr. Pinches, of the British Museum, who pointed out to me many things which might have escaped my attention, and who placed at my disposal his vast acquaintance with the texts.

If the student wish for a syllabary, I cannot but recommend that of Professor Sayce, still the best; but Mr. Pinches is preparing a very complete one, in which will be given the characters of various epochs and of all the different languages, which will be published shortly by Messrs. Trübner & Co.

G. BERTIN.

LONDON, *Sept.* 1887.

[1] Professor Sayce having kindly communicated to me advance proofs of his supplementary paper on the inscriptions of Van, I have been able to incorporate the new discoveries and post my grammar up to date (January 1888).

·SUMERO-AKKADIAN GRAMMAR.

PHONETIC.

Akkadian is written almost exclusively by means of ideograms, with or without phonetic complements; before and after certain words use is also made of determinative affixes. The phonetic pronunciation of the words, though still uncertain for some, is pretty well ascertained from the glosses given in the syllabaries and word-lists, and from comparison and analogy.

The alphabet is composed of four vowels and eighteen consonants.

The vowels are: *a*, *e*, *i*, and *u*.

The consonants may be grouped thus—

Two aspirates: ', *ġ* (*ḥ*).
Three gutturals: *g*, *k*, *ḳ*.
Three labials: *b*, *p*, *m* (*w*).
Three liquids: *n*, *l*, *r*.
Four sibilants: *s*, *š*, *z*, *ṣ*.
Three dentals: *d*, *ṭ*, *t*.

Either from the very nature of the sounds of the language, or because the characters representing these sounds were borrowed from a foreign language, the letters of each group are easily confounded: *g*, *k* and *ḳ*, *d*, *ṭ* and *t*, &c. There never was any difference made between *b* and *p*, these two letters being indifferently used for one another; *m* was never distinguished from *w*, and both letters always were written with the same characters.

At the end of a closed syllable the consonants are obscured

and take an indistinct sound, which can be transcribed by either letter of each group. The syllables *ad*, *aṭ*, and *at* give a final dental having an intermediary and uncertain sound between the three normal dentals; in the same way *ag*, *ak*, and *aḳ* give an intermediary guttural, &c. The final consonant of a word is ascertained only when followed by a vowel.

It must be noticed that *š* is, however, generally distinguished from the other sibilants.

Vocalic harmony is observed in a certain measure, but is often difficult to detect on account of the ideographic system of writing; the vowels of the suffixes or prefixes are generally assimilated to those of the noun or verb to which they are joined.

Sumerian differs from Akkadian only in its phonetic peculiarities. The letter-changes between the two dialects appear at first sight to be numerous and irregular, but are easily explained by supposing that, when the Akkadians borrowed their system of writing from the Semites, they were obliged to represent the sounds of their own language approximately by the characters giving the normal sounds of the Semitic tongues, and that the Semitic consonants represent really each several letters in Akkadian. In his transcription the scholar is obliged to follow the apparent value of the letters as given by the phonetic readings of the inscriptions, but in the following table of letter-changes each Akkadian letter is followed by the supposed real or primitive pronunciation.

' the spiritus lenis[1] remains unchanged or disappears entirely, as also sometimes in Akkadian.

ġ (*ḥ*) hard aspirate remains unchanged, or is hardened into *g* or *k*.

g normal remains unchanged or is replaced by hard *k*.
slightly aspirated is replaced by *š*.
nasal (*ñ*), like *ng* in "sing," is replaced by *m* (*w*).
dental (*ǵ*) or English *j* is replaced by *d*.
labial (*ž*) or French *j* is replaced by *b*.

[1] The spiritus lenis and forte appear to have been confounded or expressed by the same character.

k normal remains unchanged or is replaced by hard *g*.
aspirated is replaced by *š*.
ḳ normal remains unchanged or is replaced by hard *g* or *k*.
clapping is replaced by *d* or *t*.
b and *p*, these two letters, which appear to be confounded in Akkadian, are more clearly distinguished in Sumerian, but the *b* predominates.
m (*w*) remains unchanged.
n normal remains unchanged.
palatal is replaced by *l*.
aspirated is replaced by *š*.
soft is replaced by *m*.
s remains unchanged or is replaced by *š* or *ṣ*.
š normal remains unchanged.
strong is replaced by *r* or *l*.
z remains unchanged or is replaced by *ṣ*.
ṣ remains unchanged.
l remains unchanged or is replaced by *r*.
r remains unchanged or is replaced by *n*.
d normal remains unchanged or is replaced by *t*.
aspirated (soft *th*) is replaced by *ṣ* or *z*.
ṭ remains unchanged.
strong is replaced by *n*.

In the following pages the Akkadian forms will be always given; in a few cases, when the Sumerian forms are given, they will be preceded by S.

Vocalic and Consonantic Harmony.

As will be seen in the course of this grammar, vocalic harmony played probably a great part in Akkadian pronunciation, but it is very difficult for us to detect the changes, as the words are mostly written ideographically. The consonants exercised also an influence on one another; this is shown by the poetic texts, in which alliteration was largely resorted to; but as for the vocalic harmony, it is impossible to draw any rule on account of the ideographic system of writing.

NOUNS.

Nouns have not any particular forms or suffixes, the meaning and the context only show if a word is to be regarded as a noun: *ad*, "father;" *am*, "mother."

All nouns are susceptible of taking the lengthening *a-ga*, S. *a-ka*, often reduced to *ag* and *ak*, and also weakened into *aġ*.

R. As the Sumero-Akkadian is written mostly by means of ideograms, the lengthening is often added with the phonetic complement, so that the final consonant appears to be doubled:

kalam, "land;" state of prolongation, *kalam-ma-ga.*

R. The vowel of union is affected by that of the word and harmonises with it:

ud, "sun;" state of prolongation, *ud-dug.*

The most common way to lengthen the nouns is to add simply a vowel; it may be the same suffix as *ag* with the loss of the *g*:

ad, "father;" lengthening, *ad-da.*

The state of prolongation and the lengthening express emphasis, and answer in a certain measure to our article.

For the same reason, when the noun is used in the vocative, it is to be read with the lengthening, though it is not always written: *am* for *ama*, "O mother!"

The genitive is generally expressed by simple apposition: *ē-ad-da*, "the house of the father."

The dative is also often expressed by the position of the word in the sentence (see SYNTAX), but more often by a postposition.

In the accusative the nouns appear with or without the lengthening; in some cases the accusative is indicated by a postposition.

Postpositions.

Postpositions are added to the nouns to express the relations expressed in other languages by cases or by prepositions. The meanings of these postpositions are very difficult to render, as they depend in a great measure on the conception of the people, and cannot be always translated by the same prepositions of our idiom.

R. The postpositions are always added to the noun with the lengthening.

R. The vowel of the postposition is often affected by that of the noun, or dropped altogether.

The postpositions are nine in number—

-na, "in, at, to, as," primitively *en-na*.
-da, "at, in, on, with," generally without movement.
-ta, "in, from, by, for," generally with movement.
-a, "in, at," sometimes simply marks the accusative.
-ra, "to, towards, far from."
-šu (written *ku*, the pronunciation *šu* is the Sumerian which passed into Akkadian at an early date), "on, at, over," generally without movement.
-ka, "in, of" (may be another form of the preceding or the following particle).
gi, S. *ki*, "of."
gime or *ḳime*, S. *dime* (more often written *gim*, s. *dim*), "as, like."

Akkadian has no adjectives properly so called; all nouns are substantives; when they are used to express what would be an adjective in our language, they are merely put in apposition.

Gender.

The genders are not expressed by any particular forms in the nouns; there is, therefore, no gender from the grammatical point of view. Words like *ada*, "father," and *ama*, "mother," have of course a gender of meaning, but that is all; words like *gibil*, S. *kibir*, "fire" or "burning," *salim*, "peace," *gissigar*, "barrier," have really no gender.

Sometimes, but rarely, the gender is indicated by another word added to the noun: *tur-nita*, "a little one, male" = boy; *tur-sal*, "a little one, female" = girl.

Number.

There are only two numbers, the singular and the plural. The plural is, however, often not expressed, and must be detected from the context. When the plural is expressed, it is generally by simple reduplication: *kur*, "mountain;" *kur-kur*, "mountains."

R. The lengthening is placed only once after the group:

kur-kur-ra, "the mountains."

We find in the texts two other contrivances to express the plural clearly—

1°. By placing after the noun the plural of the demonstrative or third person pronoun: *dingir-ri-e-ne*, or *dingir-ri-ne-ne*, "the gods," lit. "the god, they."

2°. By placing after the noun the plural of the verb "to be:" *dum-ma-mes*, "the sons," lit. "the son, they were."

NUMERALS.

The numerals are—

1, *ge* or *aš* (for *geš*), S. *deš*.	6, *āš*.
2, *min*.	7, *īmin*.
3, *eš*.	8, *ūš*.
4, *lim*.	9, *īlim*.
5, *iā*.	

R. They can take the lengthening; often the final consonant is doubled: *mina*, *limma* or *limmu*, *īmina*, *īlimma*; *eš* and *ūš* make *ešše*, *ūšša*.

R. It is to be observed that *geš* became *a-eš* and then *aš* or that the final *š* of *geš* was lost; so we have the double form *ge* and *aš*.

R. The four last units are formed with the four first added to *iā*, "five," *āš* for *iā-aš*, *imin* for *ia-min*, &c.

The tens are—

10, *gu*, *ga*, *ū* or *ā*.	40, *nimin*.
20, *nin*, *niš*, *ban*.	50, *ninnu*.
30, *ušu*, *eš*, *ba*.	60, *šuš*, S. *muš*.

R. The forms for 10 are the produce of successive weakening.

R. The words for 30 and 40 are perhaps formed with 10 or 20 and the units *ušu* for *ū-eššē* and *eš* for *ā-eššē* (10 × 3); *nimin* for *nin-min* (20 × 2), or for *nin-nin* (20 + 20), *šuš* for *uš-uš* (30 + 30). The S. *muš* is probably from another root.

R. The forms *niš* and *ban* for 20 and *ba* for 30 are probably dialectical.

R. The numeral for 60 being taken as unit, "the soss," the words for 70, 80, and 90 were not used.

For 100 we have *me*, probably borrowed from Babylonian.

For 600, a multiple of 60, we have *ner*, also probably borrowed.

For 3600 (600 × 6), we have *sar*, lit. "multitude."

Fractions.

The word for "half" is *šuriām*.

The other fractions are expressed by *ši* placed before the numerals, generally written in ciphers—

$\frac{1}{3}$ *ši-III* or *ši-eš*.	$\frac{1}{6}$ *ši-VI* or *ši-āš*.
$\frac{1}{4}$ *ši-IV* or *ši-lim*.	$\frac{1}{10}$ *ši-X* or *ši-gu*.
$\frac{1}{5}$ *ši-V* or *ši-iā*.	

R. The soss being taken as unit, the fractions may be expressed from that standpoint, in which case special words are used—

šu-ša-na, . . $\frac{20}{60}$ or $\frac{1}{3}$, also used for 20.
ša-na-bi, . . $\frac{40}{60}$ or $\frac{2}{3}$, also used for 40.
ḳin-gu-sil-la, . $\frac{50}{60}$ or $\frac{5}{6}$, also used for 50.

Ordinal Numbers.

The numeral adjectives, or ordinal numbers, are formed by adding *gan*, s. *kam*, to the numerals, generally written in cipher—

Second, *II-gan* or *mi-na-gan.*
Third, *III-gan* or *eš-še-gan*, &c.

DEMONSTRATIVE ADJECTIVES.

There are five demonstrative pronouns or adjectives—

1°. *Am* or *ma*, primitively *ama*, "this very" (*ipse*), very emphatic pronoun.

2°. *An* or *na*, primitively *ana*, "this," pronoun of proximity (*hic*), is rarely used as a demonstrative with the nouns, no doubt because easily confounded with the postposition *-na.*

3°. *Ab* or *ba*, primitively *abi*, first pronoun of remoteness, "that" (*ille*).

4°. *A*, primitively *'e* (the aspirate is never written), second pronoun of remoteness (*iste*); it may be the adjunction of this pronoun to the nouns which in some cases appears as the lengthened forms.

5°. The compound *an-ga*, emphatic pronoun "this very" (*is ipse*).

R. The vowels of these pronouns are affected by vocalic harmony; so, for instance, the second may become *an, un, in, en*, or *na, nu, ni, ne*, according to the cases.

R. These pronouns never appear isolated, but always either suffixed to the noun or united to the verb.

PERSONAL PRONOUNS.

The personal pronouns appear to have been mostly derived from the demonstratives. The isolated pronouns are, except for the first and second persons of the singular, seldom used in the texts. They are—

1st pers.	*ga-e*, S. *ma-e*,	plur.	*ge*, S. *me*, *gu-un*, S. *mu-un*.
2nd pers.	*za-e*, S. *ṣa-e*, *ib-e*.	plur.	*e-ne*.
3rd pers.	*e-ne*, *ni* or *ni-na*, *bi*.	plur.	*e-ne-ne-ne*, *e-ne-ne*, or *e-ne*, *an-ne-ne* or *an-ne*.

These pronouns can take the postpositions, but only with certain forms.

In the singular, with the first person:

ga-da, S. *ma-da*, "with me;" *ga-ra*, S. *ma-ra*, "towards me," &c.

With the second person:

za-a-gi, S. *ṣa-a-ki*, "of thee = thine."
e-da, "with thee," *e-ta*, "from thee," &c.

With the third person:

ni-na-a, "to him," abbreviated into *na*.
bi-a, "to him," abbreviated into *ba*.
ši (for *e-šu*), "to him."

In the plural, with the first person:

ge-šu, S. *me-šu*, "to us," *ge-a*, S. *me-a*, "to us" or "us," accusative; abbreviated sometimes into *gā*, S. *mā*.

With the second person:

e-ne-a, "you," accusative.

With the third person:

an-ne-da, "with them;" *an-ne-a*, "to them" or "them."

R. As with the nouns, the postpositions are added after the lengthening; this explains the forms *gā-ra* for *ge-a-ra*, *za-a-gi* for *za-e-a-gi*, &c.

Incorporating Personal Pronouns.

Certain compound forms of the personal pronouns incorporate the whole sentence. We know these forms only for the plural; they always imply the verb "to be."

1st pers. *ge-en-ne* . . . . *en*, "we are."
an-ne . . . . . *en.*
2nd pers. *ge-en-zi* . . . . *en*, or *ge-zi* . . . . *en*, "you are."
an-zi. . . . . . *en.*
ab-zi. . . . . . *en.*
3rd pers. *an-ne* . . . . . *en*, "they are."
an-ne-ne . . . . *en.*

For the singular the emphatic personal pronouns are used with the verb "to be."

ga-e . . . . *me-en*, "I am;" *za-e* . . . . *me-en*, "thou art."

Pronominal Suffixes.

The possessive is expressed by the emphatic pronoun under a certain form put in apposition after the noun, that is, suffixed to the lengthened form:

dib-ba-gu, S. *gub-ba-mu*, "the doing of me" = "my doing."
ē-a-zu, "the house of thee" = "thy house."
šu-a-ni, "the hand of him" = "his hand."

For the third person the pronoun *bi* is also used, but is more often to be translated by the demonstrative:

lu-bi, "his man" or "that man."

As we say in English "my man" for "this man I spoke of."

The plural is not generally expressed in the possessive pronouns; when this is done, it is like in the noun by means of the plural of demonstrative pronoun:

ē-a-zu-ne-ne, lit. "the house of thee these" = "your house."

We have therefore for the possessive suffixes the following table:

1st pers. *-gu*, S. *-mu*, "my" or "our;"	emphatic plur.	*-gu-ne-ne*, "our."	
2nd pers. *-zu*, S. *-ṣu*, "thy" or "your,"	„	*-zu-ne-ne*, "your."	
3rd pers. *-ni*, "his" or "their,"	„	*-ni-ne-ne*, "their."	
		-e-ne-ne.	
		-e-ne.	

R. On account of the vocalic harmony, the pronominal forms, such as *an-ne*, *an-ne-en*, *ab-zi-en*, &c., can become *en-ne*, *in-ne*, *un-ne*, *en-ne-en*, *in-ne-en*, &c.

Interrogative Pronouns.

A-ba, "who;" *a-na*, "which, what;" *e-še* or *iš-en*, "who, which."

Indefinite Pronouns.

Na-mi, "some one;" *nig*, "something," lit. "a thing;" abbreviated also in *ig*, S. *ag* or *ī*; *nu-uš* and *nu-ub-da*, "no one."

Relative Pronouns.

Nig, "which," lit. "a thing."

For "beings" the demonstrative emphatic pronouns are used.

Hyperbolic Pronouns.

Sometimes nouns are used instead of personal pronouns, as *lu*, "man," for "I;" *ka*, "mouth," for "thou," &c. As in the Semitic tongues, "head" is used with the possessive suffixes for the emphatic pronouns.

R. With these words there is no localisation more than with the demonstratives; *lu* is used for "he" as well as for "I," and may be also used for "thou."

Nouns with the possessive adjectives are also used: *im-zu*, "thy breath" = "thou."

R. The use of those hyperbolic pronouns is not restricted to personal pronouns, but they may be used for indefinite and other pronouns: *lu-na*, "the *or* this man," for "somebody," and also for "who?"

VERB.

All verbs may have the active or passive, transitive or intransitive meaning, as some of our verbs: "to look," actively "to fix the eye on something," passively "to appear;" so *gin*, act. "to fix," pass. "to be fixed," *i.e.*, "to stand."

R. Properly speaking, the verb has always a nominal meaning; it is only its position in the sentence, the context, or the addition of pronominal suffixes and particles, which show how it is to be translated.

As the noun, the verbal theme or stem appears under two forms—the bare form and the lengthened form.

The lengthening is added exactly as with the noun:

dun, "to go;" lengthened form, *dun-na*.

The lengthening was primitively a demonstrative pronoun suffixed to the noun, and for this reason it represents with a word used as verb the action as present:

dun, "a going," that is, the action of going being completed, which consequently expresses the past, "a having gone" or "went."

dun-na, "the *or* this going," that is, the action in the act of being performed, which consequently expresses the present, "a being going."

R. The verbal stem, bare or lengthened, may be used without any pronoun, the bare form having the force of past and the lengthened of present or future.

The plural is often not expressed, being implied by the subject given in the sentence; but when the writers wished to express it emphatically, it was done by means of *eše*, a disused word meaning "many," abridged into *eš*, and added to the stem with the lengthening:

gar, "to do," "doing," or "he did;" plur. *gar-ri-eš*, "to do (many)," "doings," or "they did."

R. The vowel of *eš* is often assimilated :

šum-mu-uš, "they gave."

When the lengthened form is to be used, the plural, if expressed, is formed by adding the plural of the second demonstrative pronoun :

gar-ra, "the doing," or "he does;" plur. *gar-ri-e-ne-ne*, "these doings," or "they do."

Reduplication.

Reduplication gives to the stem a factitive or causative meaning :

gi, "to turn;" *gi-gi*, "to cause to turn" or "to send away."

In many cases, however, it does not alter the primitive meaning, and only expresses emphasis :

gi-gi-e-ne, "they are turning about."

Precative.

The precative is expressed by the prefix *ġa* :

ġa-gar, "may he do," lit. "be a doing."

R. The vowel of this prefix may be changed under the influence of vocalic harmony, and the prefix becomes *ġe-*, *gi-*, *ġu-*. In some cases the consonant is weakened into *g* : *ga-*, *ge-*, *gi-*, *gu-*, and is even dropped, or the prefix is reduced to *a-* :

ga-gar, "may he do."
a-ba-ni-in-gin, "may he return to it."

Negative.

The negation with the verb is expressed by the prefixes *nu-* or *la-* (this last is very rare, and may only be but a dialectical variation) :

nu-zu, "not to know."
la-gin, "not to fix."

R. Through the vocalic harmony the prefix can become *na-*, rarely *ne* or *ni;* before the labials *b*, *p*, and *m* it is sometimes *nam-*.

INCORPORATION.

The verbal stem can incorporate not only pronouns representing all the various elements of the sentence, but also the particles.

The incorporated pronouns are forms of the five demonstratives modified through vocalic harmony.

The first pronoun appears under the forms *ma*, *mu*, *mi*, *me*, or *am*, *um*, *im;* it is always placed first before all the other incorporated pronouns or particles, never expresses the subject, and often represents an adverb, an indirect object, or an expression modifying or explaining the meaning of the verbal stem.

The second or pronoun of proximity appears under the forms *na*, *nu*, *ni*, *ne*, or *an*, *un*, *in*, *en*, and after *m*, the *n* being assimilated, *-ma*, *-mu*, *-mi*, *-me*. It may represent the subject or object, direct or indirect, or even as the first pronoun, an adverb, &c.

The third pronoun or first of remoteness appears under the forms *ba*, *bu*, *bi*, *be*, or *ab*, *ub*, *ib*, *eb;* the use of it is the same as for the second.

The fourth pronoun or second of remoteness appears under the form *a*, *u*, *i*, *e;* it is easily absorbed by the vowel of the next element in the incorporation, and even disappears entirely; the presence of a postpositive particle without a pronoun or the vocalic alteration of the other pronoun shows that it once existed in the group.

The fifth or compound emphatic pronoun appears under the forms *an-ga*, *un-ga*, *in-ga*, *en-ga;* sometimes the *n* is dropped, and we have *a-ga*, &c. Like the first pronoun, it never represents the subject, but the object or an adverb, &c., on which the writer wants to lay a special stress.

R. As a rule, these pronouns represent in the incorporation either a singular or a plural; sometimes, but rarely, the plural is represented by the syllable *-ne* suffixed to the incorporated pronoun.

The incorporated particles are the same as the postpositions added to the nouns, but only the six first are used in the incorporation:

(1.) The first appears under the forms *na*, *nu*, *ni*, *ne*, or *an*, *un*, *in*, *en*, and by assimilation *ma*, *mu*, *mi*, *me*.

(2.) The second under the forms *da* and *di*.

(3.) The third under the forms *ta* and *te*.

(4.) The fourth under the forms *ra* and *ri*.

(5.) The fifth under the forms *ši* and *še*.

(6.) The sixth under the form *a*, but often disappears altogether.

R. The particles are suffixed to the incorporated pronouns which represents in the verbal form the noun with the postposition of the sentence.

R. They have the same force and meaning as the postpositions added to the noun, but do not always in the incorporation correspond to the postpositions used in the sentences. The incorporated *na* may correspond to the postposition *da*, the incorporated *ta* to *gime*, &c.

The incorporated pronouns represent the various elements of the sentence irrespectively of their gender, and often number, and of their person; they only represent the words in their relation to each other in space or time. The subject will be treated in the syntax. We have here to consider these pronouns only under their grammatical aspect; to do this it is more convenient to use the following abbreviations:—

s = subject; it is placed always at the end of the incorporated group, that is, prefixed direct to the verb.

o = object, that is, the direct object of the verb or accusative; it comes next to the subject when there is no indirect object.

i = indirect object, which always has an incorporated particle; it is placed between the direct object and the subject.

p = particle, that is, the incorporated particle which governs the indirect object; it naturally always follows the incorporated pronoun representing the indirect object.

c = complement explicative, that is, the incorporated pronoun representing in the verbal form the adverb, locution, or expression explaining, limiting, or specialising the meaning of the stem.

v = verbal stem, that is, the verb or noun used as such.

If I wish to say, "I gave with pleasure the book to my brother," the verbal form may contain incorporated pronouns representing every element of the sentence :—I = *s*, with pleasure = *c*, the book = *o*, to = *p*, my brother = *o*. We will have as verbal form c-o-i-p-s-v, *sic-illud-hunc-ad-ego-dedi.*

Except the first pronoun (*ma*, &c.), and the fifth or emphatic compound pronoun (*an-ga*, &c.), any of the pronouns may represent any of these grammatical relations.

The incorporation is not always complete; only part of the sentence may be represented; often the subject is omitted, or the object, direct or indirect, and also the complement; but if two or more of the sentence-elements are represented, the incorporated pronouns keep the relative position of the grammatical relation they represent.

There are therefore fifteen possible forms :—

Complete form	c-o-i-p-s-v,	all the elements being represented.
Incomplete (1st degree)	o-i-p-s-v, c—i-p-s-v, c-o——s-v, c-o-i-p—v,	three elements only being represented.
,, (2nd degree)	i-p-s-v, o——s-v, c———s-v, o-i-p—v, c—i-p—v, c-o———v,	two elements only being represented.
,, (3rd degree)	s-v, i-p—v, o———v, c———v,	one element only being represented.

R. All these combinations may take place with the stem either bare or lengthened, and also with their plural forms when the subject of the verb is a plural; but often the verbal stem is not in the plural with a plural subject.

R. When the prefix of the precative or the negative is used with a verbal stem with an incorporated group, it is placed first; so the incorporated group is placed between this prefix or negative and the verbal stem.

Emphatic Imperative.

A kind of emphatic imperative is formed by prefixing to the verbal form the copula *ū* or *u*, which in this case may be translated by "then," "indeed," or "ha!" and the complement is always expressed by the first incorporated pronoun: *u-me-ni-šar*, "thou repeat then so."

Pronouns Suffixed to the Stem.

Part or the whole of the incorporation may be placed after the verbal stem. When only one pronoun, as *am*, *en*, *ib*, &c., is suffixed, it may be considered as a demonstrative determining the stem itself, and for this reason represents, in a certain measure, the subject. When the whole group of the incorporation is suffixed, its elements keep the same position, v-c-o-i-p-s; therefore the complement and the objects, direct and indirect, with the particle are practically incorporated between the stem and the pronoun-subject to be considered in this case as a demonstrative.

R. The suffixed incorporated group may offer all the same combinations as when prefixed.

R. When more than one element of the incorporation is suffixed, none can be prefixed.

Compound Verbal Stems.

The compound verbal stems, that is, those formed by a word used as a verb and a noun simple or compound, incorporate the pronouns and particles between their two elements:

igi-šum, "to look," lit. "to give eye,"
gab-ri, "oppose," lit. "to turn the breast,"

make

[1]igi-[2]im-[3]ma-[4]an-[5]šum, "he took to him," lit. "[4]he [5]gave the [1]eye [3]to [2]him."

gab-im-ma-an-ri, "he opposed him," lit. "he turned the breast to him."

R. When the verbal stem is composed of more than two elements, only one, the last, is the verb; the others form one word, which is placed before the incorporation: *šu-gar—gi*, "to revenge," composed of *šu-gar* and *gi;* the incorporation is placed between *gar* and *gi*.

R. The first element may be considered as an explicative complement, and as such placed at the head of the incorporation; but when the pronouns and particles are suffixed, it keeps its place before the verb.

ADVERBS.

Properly speaking, there are no adverbs; these are expressed by means of nouns with a demonstrative pronoun or a postposition:

šur-bi or *šur-ra-na*, "strongly;" *agi-gim*, "like dark water."
ki-ta, "on the earth" with movement; *u-kur-šu*, "in another day = at a future time;" *u-bi-a*, "then," &c.

CONJUNCTION.

The only conjunction is the copula *u* * "and," rarely "or." Sometimes postpositions are used for the copula, *ana-ki-ta*, "heaven and earth," lit. "heaven earth—with."

* It is read *ša* by some.

SYNTAX.

I. Words.

All nouns in their bare or lengthened forms may be used for the masculine and feminine singular or plural.

When the genitive is expressed by apposition, the regent is placed first, and the governed word only takes the lengthening: *ĕ-ad-da*, "the house of the father."

R. In a few expressions, probably archaic, the order is interverted: *ana-šaga*, "the sky's middle."

The noun taken as adjective follows the word it qualifies: *ku-azag-ga*, "the metal shining" or "bright metal" (= silver).

When the noun expresses the person for whom the action is done, it may take no postposition, but simply be placed at the head of the sentence (see further Syntax of Sentence).

The postpositions are added to the lengthened forms of the noun or compound expression; though not always written in the texts, it must be supplied in reading: *sil-na*, for *sila-na*, "in the street;" *an-šag-šu*, for *ana-šaga-šu*, "in the middle of the sky."

The noun in the accusative or as direct object may be in the bare or lengthened forms, but sometimes the accusative relation is indicated by a postposition: *-na*, *-da*, or *-a*.

The demonstrative adjectives suffixed to the nouns do not always indicate relation of distance; they also serve to denote the instrument or the manner: *šu-bi*, "with the hand;" *sil-la-am*, "in the street;" *ner-ri-ni*, "with the foot."

The emphatic personal pronouns, as subjects, are generally placed at the beginning of the sentence (see Syntax of Sentence).

They may be used as objects.

For the use of the incorporating pronouns we have the following example: *me-en-ne uru-šu ġa-ni-dudu-en*, precative form, "may we be going to the city."

The interrogative *aba*, "who," *ana*, "what," "which," are always placed at the beginning of the sentence.

The verbal stem is always placed at the end of the sentence. When it is placed in the middle, it is to be considered as an adjective or participle.

The incorporated pronouns never distinguish the person; the same form is used to represent either the first, second, or third person.

In some texts, however, there is a tendency to use the pronouns of remoteness for the second person (comp. the use of *iste* in Latin).

The relations expressed by the pronoun of proximity and the two pronouns of remoteness are not always relations of distance; but they indicate also (1) the comparative relations of the various elements of the sentence as to time (if the action was performed at some period previous to the narration, or is to be performed later on, the remote pronouns will be used); (2) the comparative importance of the various elements represented in the incorporation as to the performance of the action.

When translating a text, it is, therefore, to be considered if the author had in view to indicate, with the three different pronouns, a relation of distance, of time, or of importance. In the first case, the pronouns may in a certain measure represent a relation of persons, like in Latin, *na* (*hic*) = "I or me," *ba* (*ille*) = "he or him" and *e* (*iste*) = "thou or thee," but not necessarily, as the relation of distance may be considered from the point of view of the performance of the action; so, if the subject is a first or second person, the near pronoun would represent the first or second, and the two others may represent the person of the object, direct or indirect.

The first and fifth pronouns never express a relationship, but only represent the element to which the speaker wishes to draw special attention; they never represent the subject.

The various elements of the sentence are sometimes represented by the same incorporated pronoun, which is, in that case, generally *na* more often than *ba*.

As a rule, the subject and object are represented by different pronouns.

With the particles *ta* and *ra*, the subject and indirect object are never represented by the same pronoun.

The desire for clearness or emphasis seems to have guided the authors in the use of a complete or incomplete incorporation.

The presence of the incorporated particles are, with some verbal stems, indispensable to determine the meaning:

> *ê* is "to go," with the incorporated *ta*, "to send away."
> *ib-ta-an-ê*, "he send (him) away from it."
> *lal* is "to weigh," with *na*, "to weigh for" or "to pay."
> *in-na-an-lal*, "he weighed to him" or "he paid to him."

When one of the incorporated pronouns, or the whole of the group, is placed after the verbal stem, it gives to it a participial force.

All verbal forms, with complete or incomplete incorporation, may be used as imperatives. All the forms, as well as the precative and the imperative proper, seem to be used indifferently; it may, however, be stated, that the precative expresses a wish, the simple imperative an order, and the emphatic imperative a prayer or entreaty.

The copula *u* is placed either between the two nouns to be united, or after the second, like *que* in Latin.

II. Syntax of Sentence.

The order in which the words are placed together to form a sentence is not the same as that of the incorporated pronouns which represent them in the verbal form, and not so regular. This irregularity, when it is not through poetical license, is, however, only apparent, as the position of the words in the sentence depends on the point of view from which they are grammatically considered.

To understand the Sumero-Akkadian ideology, it is indispensable to analyse the elements or members of the sentence as they are conceived in this language. These elements can be classed under seven different headings:

1. The subject (*s*), or nominative.

2. The object (*o*), or accusative.

3. The indirect object (*i*).

4. The motive or reason (*r*), for which the action is performed.

5. The complement (*c*), that is, the manner in which the action is performed.

6. The determinative (*d*), generally expressed by what is called by grammarians the adverb or adverbial locution, and marking either the time (*dt*), place (*dp*), or state (*ds*), in which the action is performed.

7. The verb (*v*), or the verbal stem, with or without the pronouns and particles.

To these we may add the qualificative (*q*), which is a secondary element, explaining or specifying primitive elements, subject, object, &c., and which may be either a noun-adjective, a noun in the genitive, or with postposition, or even a whole sentence, and always follows immediately the word it qualifies.

To give an example in our language, if we say, "Yesterday the king, to recompense him, gave magnanimously to the soldier a sword of honour," it is analysed thus: yesterday = *d*, the king = *s*, to recompense him = *r*, gave = *v*, magnanimously = *c*, a sword of honour = *o*, to the soldier = *i*; giving the formula d-s-r-v-c-o-i. In this sentence we have besides "of honour" = *q*, qualifying "a sword."

In Sumero-Akkadian the formula would be d-r-s-o-i-c-v; that is, 1st, the determinative or locution marking time, place, or state; 2nd, the expression, stating the reason or motive of the action; 3rd, the subject; 4th, the object; 5th, the indirect object; 6th, the complement or expression explaining how the action is done; and 7th, the verb.

R. Sentences containing all the elements are never found, but the elements expressed keep the same relative position. In the case of a narration or speech, some are naturally often understood; as, for instance, the subject, which is not repeated in every sentence. The same happens also for the other elements.

R. It is evident that in every sentence the different words or expressions might be viewed in different ways, and their position altered according to the view taken by the writer. For instance, "magnanimously" might be considered as a qualificative either "to recompense," the reason of the action, or to "king," the subject, and "recompense" might be considered as a qualificative to "sword of honour" and expressed "as recompense," &c. It is these different possible conceptions which give flexibility to the language.

R. The complement, in some cases, is really qualificative to the verb, and the word which plays this part may be considered in a certain measure as forming a compound stem with the verb.

R. The three kinds of determinatives (adverbial expressions) (*d*), marking the time (*dt*), the place (*dp*), and the state (*ds*), might be found in the same sentence.

R. The fixed place assigned to each member of the sentence explains how the postpositions are often neglected, as the position of the members of the sentence is sufficient to mark their relation and the part they play.

A complete sentence would contain nine members, disposed according to the following formula: dt-dp-ds-r-s-o-i-c-v. We therefore can obtain 511 combinations, thus:

Complete sentence, all the members being expressed.

Incomplete (1st degree), one member missing, 9 combinations.

(2nd „),	two members	„ 36	„
(3rd „),	three „	„ 84	„
(4th „),	four „	„ 126	„
(5th „),	five „	„ 126	„
(6th „),	six „	„ 84	„
(7th „),	seven „	„ 36	„
(8th „),	eight „	„ 9	„

Any sentence which is not complete, that is, which does not contain the nine different members, must belong to one of these eight classes.

R. The qualificative is not by itself a member of the sentence, but only forms part of a member with the word or expression it qualifies.

R. The particles incorporated, the prefixes of the negative and precative are to be considered as qualifications to the verb.

R. When the verb has a neuter meaning, there is naturally no direct object, and the sentence therefore cannot be complete.

R. In the texts it would seem that there is sometimes a transposition of the three first terms (*dt*, *dp*, and *ds*); this comes from a confusion in the mind of the authors. The determinative of state may indeed in many cases be considered as a determinative of time or of place.

R. In Sumero-Akkadian, as in the other languages, the complete sentences are avoided, as they would render the periods heavy and intricate. For quickness and clearness, authors prefer to break up the period in small sentences more or less connected; for this reason most of the sentences found in the texts belong to the last classes.

R. Sentences of the last class (incomplete 8th degree) are only imperatives or vocatives used alone.

dingir-ra-ñi-ir lugal-la e mu-ne-en-du, "for his god the king built a house," incomplete 5th degree, formula r-s-o-v.

ib-ba-bi-ta dingir ki-gi kia ba-an-du-ne-es, "in this (for their) anger the gods of the earth go on the earth," incomplete 5th degree, formula ds-s-i-v: *ki-gi*, "of the earth," is qualificative to the subject *dingir*.

an-bara nig-si-sa gu-bi ma-ra-an-ri, "the Sun-god sets the right thing by (a sign of) his head," incomplete 5th degree, formula s-o-c-v.

as ǵul galla-gim lu-ra ba-ni-in-gin, "the demon-like curse is fixed on the man," incomplete 6th degree, formula s-i-v: *galla-ǵim* is qualificative to the subject.

u-ebur-ra-ka ašaga gis-ab-ur-ra, "at the time of work he ploughs with wood (*i.e.*, rakes) the field," incomplete 6th degree, formula dt-o-v: *gis* forms with the verb a compound stem.

Similarly in the following example:

ašaga a-ib-ta-an-de, "he gives water (*i.e.*, he waters) the field," incomplete 7th degree, formula o-v: *a* forms with *de* a compound stem.

Complex Periods.

Sometimes some members of the sentence are composed of another sentence, which is then secondary or incidental, and the qualificative may also be expressed by a secondary or incidental sentence.

In these two cases the secondary sentence keeps the place of the member it represents or follows the member it qualifies.

The secondary sentence is either placed in apposition, its relation to the principal sentence is then shown only by its position, or takes a postfix which governs the whole of it, or its verb takes the participial form.

R. Several secondary sentences may follow one another united or not by the copula, but as a rule in the second case they represent different numbers of the sentence.

Secondary or incidental sentence in apposition:

azag-tag-a-ni in-na-an-še | *ur-ra-na-nam ne-en-gir* | *e-ta ib-ta-an-ê*, "he gave to him her dowry; he bound it in his girdle; he sent him away from the house." The principal sentence is the last; the two first play the part of determinatives; the first being considered as marking the time (*dt*) "when he had given to him," &c., and the second the state (*ds*), "having bound it," &c.

Participial secondary or incidental sentence:

salmi-ni-in-dug-ga | *te-bi nu-ub-ra-ʿ ağ mi-ni-in-dim*, "a woman having spoken to him, he withheld himself from her." The first sentence is secondary, and plays the part of the determinative, marking the time or the state (*dt* or *ds*).

Adverbial secondary or incidental sentence:

a-šaga al-sal-ta ba-ab-ag-ta | *gis-gan-uru mu-šar-a-ta ba-ab-ur-ra*, "after he had possession of the field, he drives palings in the furrow." The first sentence, which plays the part of the determinative of time (*dt*), has the postposition *ta* governing the whole of it. This postposition is the one mostly used to form determinative or adverbial secondary sentences.

Qualificative secondary or incidental sentence:

u-bi-a el-lil-la | *dim-bi gis-ne-in-du-a* | *enim šaga-bi-šu ba-an-bu-i*, "then Bel, who heard this news, took the matter at heart." The secondary sentence plays the part of an adjective.

ASSYRO-BABYLONIAN GRAMMAR.

PHONETIC.

THE alphabet is the same as for Sumero-Akkadian, but the sound of each letter is more fixed.

The vowels may be long or short; *ă*, *ĭ*, and *ŭ* are weak vowels, and *ĭ* is the weakest, often taking the sound of the French mute *e*; the other three weak vowels have also a tendency to be obscured to the same extent, and often they are written only, on account of the syllabic system of writing, to give a consonant which could not be written alone, just as in Ethiopian. The vowel *e* is never weak; when weakened it becomes *ĭ*; *ē* and *ī* are confounded. Long vowels are sometimes, but not always, represented by repeating the vowel, as *lu-u* for *lū*; *i-e* stands often for *ī* or *ē*. Long vowels are found even in closed syllables, where there is nothing to show us that they are such: *lut* for *lūt*, *tir* for *tīr*, &c. When two vowels meet they are often contracted: *ai*, *ae* and *ea* become *ē*, *ia* becomes *ī*, *ie* and *ei* become *ē*. The vowel *u* absorbs all the others and becomes long, so that *au*, *ua*, *iu*, *ui*, *ue*, *eu* become *ū*. In some cases, however, *ue* or *eu* are represented by *ē*; hence *ui* may become *ī* for *e*.

A weak vowel not accentuated, following an open syllable and followed by a single consonant and vowel, is generally dropped: *belĭt* and *beltu*, "lady."

The vowel *e* is generally employed to lengthen a syllable: *šarrie* for *šarrī*; so *šarrū* has passed through *šarrue*.

The length of a long vowel is sometimes represented by the doubling of the following consonant: *amma* for *āma*, *atta* for *āta*, *illi* for *īli*, &c. Sometimes the addition of *n* or *m* is used for the same purpose; *an* or *am* may therefore stand for *ā*. It is probable that in those cases it represented a nasalisation. The *n* is used in preference before a dental, and *m* before a labial, but both are found before other consonants.

The doubling of consonants was by analogy often represented by lengthening the previous vowel or by placing *n* or *m* before the consonant to be doubled.

The aspirate ' indicates sometimes that the preceding vowel is long, and also represents a primitive nasalisation.

Very often the aspirate ' is not represented at all by the writing; so when two vowels follow one another, we may suppose an aspirate: *ta-ā-ru* for *ta'āru*, *tairu* for *ta'iru*.

Sometimes *ḳ* and *g* are confounded: *ḳatu* and *gatu*, "hand;" also *k* and *ḳ*: *kibit* and *ḳibit*, "command," *ḳ* becomes usually *k* before *i* and *e*.

In some cases *m* (*w*) seems to have grown out of a *u*: *abumi* for *abūi*, "my father;" in others, *m* is weakened into *u*.

Consonants of the same organ are sometimes assimilated: *erum-ma*, "he went," for *erub-ma*.

Before a guttural and a sibilant *m* often becomes *n*: *dunḳu* for *dumḳu*, "lucky;" *ḥanša* for *ḥamša*, "five."

After a guttural *t* becomes *ṭ* or *d*: *aḳṭirib* for *aḳtirib*, "I approached."

In the same way after *m* (and also, but rarely, after *b* and *p*) *t* becomes *d*: *amdaḥiṣ* for *amtaḥiṣ*, "I fought."

When *n* comes into contact with another consonant it is generally assimilated: *šattu* for *šantu*, "year;" *ibbu* for *inbu*, "he proclaimed."

Sometimes *l* is assimilated when it comes into contact with a sibilant or an *r*.

Sometimes *r* is assimilated: *annu* for *arnu*, "sin;" *kussu* for *kursu*, "throne."

The two sibilants *ṣ* and *z* are sometimes interchanged: *irzitu* and *irṣitu*, "earth."

When two sibilants meet, they have a tendency to be assimilated or to be changed in *ss*.

When *š* meets a *t* it is changed into *l*: *ḥamiltu* for *ḥamištu*, "five;" the other sibilants assimilate the *t*.

When *t* is followed by a sibilant the two consonants become *ss*: *mussu* for *mut-šu*, "her husband."

Two *ss* become *s* simple: *balasun* for *balassun* (which is itself for *balat-šun*), "their life."

These letter-changes and phonetic peculiarities are most important, and must always be borne in mind when deciphering a text; they will explain the apparent irregularities.

Often, however, the scribes appear to have retained the etymological orthography, though no doubt it was read according to the phonetic laws of the language. We find *ḳat-šu*, *balat-šu*, &c., which was probably read *ḳasu*, *balasu*, &c., according to the rule given above.

Vocalic and Consonantic Harmony.

There appears to have been a tendency to harmonise all the vowels of each word and to bring them to one type. The stem EPS makes *epēsu* (instead of *eapāsu*); *šalaštu* makes *šelalti* (probably read *šelelti*). This harmonic tendency was carried even to the consonants, and often a consonant is altered by the presence of another in the same word, though separated by other letters: *iddidin* for *intadin*. The Babylonians had a liking for accumulation of the same consonants, and as result of assimilation we get themes like ZZZ, BBB, &c.

Accentuation.

The accent is almost invariably on the penultimate, and exactly as in Italian, when the penultimate has a weak vowel the accent is thrown on the ante-penultimate. The accent is often represented by doubling the initial consonant of the next syllable, and for this reason accent is often confounded with length of the vowel.

The suffixes and the enclitics generally throw the accent on the preceding syllable. The word which receives the accent from the enclitic seldom loses its own, but sometimes it is thrown farther back; the word has therefore two accents.

TRILITERISM.

Though Assyro-Babylonian was written with syllabic signs, it offers to a great extent the same phenomena exhibited by the other Semitic tongues and produced by the triliterism. As explained by the late Professor Palmer,[1] the Semites treated the fundamental letters of every root as algebraic elements, assuming that every root was composed of three letters: XYZ. When one of the *radical* letters was a vowel, the root was called *weak* of the first, second, or third radical, as the case might be. When the three radicals were consonantic, the root or stem was called *strong*.

To preserve the triliteral harmony of the words when they have only two consonants, either one of them is doubled, or one of the vowels is lengthened to represent the supposed weak radical. The Babylonian and Ninevite scribes have often shown a certain hesitation between the two alternatives; so we have *rabbu* (supposed root RBB) and *rabū* (supposed root RBU). There was also some hesitation as to the place of the weak radical: *ataru* (ATR) and *tāru* (TAR). Sometimes the weak radical is supposed to have been primitively an aspirate, and the scribe re-establishes it: *ta'aru* (T'R).

For the same reason the derivatives of weak stems are often treated as primitive, and such is the origin of many of the so-called triliteral strong verbs: *šakānu*, "to place," is a Shaphel of *kānu*, "to stand."

FORMS OF THE WORDS.

The parts of the speech may be divided into three: nouns (and adjectives), verbs, and particles.

There are only two genders, masculine and feminine, and three numbers, singular, dual, and plural.

[1] See his abridged Arabic Grammar, p. 59.

NOUNS AND ADJECTIVES.

As nouns and adjectives follow in most cases the same rules of formation, it is as well to treat them together.

All nouns and adjectives have two forms, one short, which is considered as primitive and called *construct state*, because used when the word is constructed with another forming with it one expression; the other longer, which we call the *casal form*, has three different endings, answering to the three cases of Arabic.

In the construct state the word has no foreign element attached to it: *nakir*, "enemy;" *zumur*, "body."

When the noun ends in a vowel this is often dropped: *ab*, "father."

When the noun ends in a double consonant (as in the words having the same consonant as second and third radical or those formed by the doubling of the last radical), this double letter is expressed by a single one: *šar*, "king" (for *šarr*); *nudun*, "dowry" (for *nudunn*).

The casal form is terminated in *u* for the subjective, in *i* for the dependent, and in *a* for the objective case.

Sometimes the casal form is simply the noun in the construct state with these vowels added to it: *nakir*, subjective case *nakiru*.

When the last vowel of the word in the construct state is weak and unaccented, it is generally dropped: *zumur*, dependent case *zumri*.

When the word is a noun derived from a root weak of the third radical, the vowel of the casal form is long: *ab*, subj. *abū*; dependent *abī*; obj. *abā*.

The words which drop one of their double consonant in the construct state restore it in the casal form: *šar*, subj. case *šarru*; *nudun*, dependent case *nudunni*.

The feminine in the construct state is formed from the masculine by the suffix *at* or *it* substituted to the vowel of the casal form. Vowel harmony seems to rule the choice of one or the other suffix: *kalbu*, "dog," fem. *kalbat; bēlu*, "lord," fem. *bēlit.*

In the casal form the vowel preceding the *t* of the suffix is sometimes preserved, but more often is dropped; in this case the vowel preceding the last consonant of the word must be restored if it be one containing three consonants, and in words having a double consonant like *šarrat* the *a* of the suffix is necessarily maintained; *kalbat* makes subj. case *kalbatu; šarrat*, subj. case *šarratu; aḥat*, sister, subj case *aḥatu;* but *bēlit* makes subj. case *bēltu.*

Dual.

The suffix of the dual was primitively *ăn*, but it became *ā* in the course of time, though the two endings are found:

> *šaptu*, "the lip;" *šaptan* and *šaptā*, "the two lips."
> *uznu*, "the ear;" *uznā*, "the two ears."

Plural.

A primitive way to express the plural, imitated perhaps from Akkadian, is by reduplication. It is, however, of a very limited use. When the word was polysyllabic, only one syllable was repeated:

> *mu*, "water;" plur. *mami.*
> *šamu*, "sky;" plur. *šamame.*

The plural was more often formed by lengthening the vowel of the casal form, the lengthening being made by adding the vowel *e*. We ought to have: subj. *ue*, dep. *ie*, and obj. *ae;* but the vowels are often assimilated, and we find subj. *ū*, dep. *ī*, obj. *ā*. In general it is the vowel *e* which has absorbed the other, and we have *e* for all cases of the plural. Sometimes the same word is found with the two forms *umū* and *ume*, "days."

Another way of forming the plural is by the suffix *nu*, generally weakened into *ni*, added to the casal form of the singular. We might expect forms in *uni*, *ini*, *ani*, or *unu*, *inu*, *anu*, but the form in *ani* is almost exclusively used, and is found side by side with the plural in *ie*: *šarrani* and *šarrie*, "kings."

The plural of the feminine is formed by changing *at* into *āte*, sometimes *āti*, very rarely *ātu*.

This formation probably originated from adding the feminine suffix to the plural of the masculine; *āte* would be for *ā-ate*. We might then expect the forms *ūtu* for *ū-atu*, *ātu* for *ā-atu*, *ītu* for *ī-atu*, but the forms in *āte* and *āti* only are preserved; the final *e* or *i* is, no doubt, by analogy to the masculine plural in *e*.

The words taking *itu* in the singular make *īti* or *ēti* in the plural: *šarrāte*, "queens;" *bēlieti*, "ladies."

The forms in *ūtu* or *ūti* are applied to form the plural of adjectives in the masculine, as *ilani rabuti*, "the great gods."

The form in *utu* is used to form abstracts, which are used as singular nouns, and have no plural: *šarrutu*, "kingship" or "royalty."

The construct state is generally the same as the casal form. In a few rare cases, however, it is formed by dropping the final consonant.

Mimation and Emphatic State.

Primitively the casal form was terminated by an *m*, and was subj. *um*, dep. *im*, obj. *am*. Subj. *šiprum*, "the message;" dep. *irṣitim*, "the earth;" obj. *ḥirram*, "the free-born child."

These mimated forms were soon more weakened still, and the *m* dropped was replaced by a simple aspirate; it is what we call the emphatic state (see Syntax), to distinguish it from the mimation: obj. *kašpa'*, "the money."

NUMERALS.

The numerals have two genders; they are from one to ten.

	Masculine.			*Feminine.*		
1.	*ešten,*	c.f.	*eštānu.*	*edit,*	c.f.	*editu.*
2.	*šina,*	„	*šinū.*	*šinat,*	„	*šinatu.*
3.	*šalaš,*	„	*šalšu.*	*šalšat,*	„	*šalaštu* or *šalaltu.*
4.	*arba,*	„	*arbū.*	*arbat,*	„	*arbatu.*
	or *arbaʿ,*	„	*arbaʿu* or *arbau.*	or *irbit,*	„	*irbittu.*
5.	*ḥamiš,*	„	*ḥamšu* or *ḥanšu.*	*ḥamšat,*	„	*ḥamiltu.*
6.	*šiš,*	„	*šiššu.*	*šiššat,*	„	*šiššatu.*
7.	*siba,*	„	*sibau* or *sibū.*	*sibit,*	„	*sibitu* or *sibittu.*
8.	*šamna,*	„	*šamnu.*	*šamnat,*	„	*šamnatu.*
9.	*tiš* or *tiša,*	„	*tisū.*	*tisit,*	„	*tišitu* or *tišittu.*
10.	*ešer,*	„	*ešru.*	*ešrit,*	„	*ešritu.*
				or *ešerit,*	„	*ešeritu.*

The numeral for "twenty" is the dual of "ten;" the other tens are formed from the units by lengthening the vowel of the casal form, but they are always vocalised in *ā*:

20. *ešrā* (dual of 10).	60. *šišā.*
30. *šelašā.*	70. *sibā.*
40. *irbā* or *irbaʿia.*	80. *šamnā.*
50. *ḥansā.*	90. *tišā.*

The word for 100 is *me* invariable; *šina me,* 200.

From 11 to 19 the units are placed, as in Latin, before ten: *ešten-ešrit,* "eleven;" and the compounds are considered as forming only one word: *ḥamiššerit,* "fifteen."

Numeral Adjectives.

The ordinal or numeral adjectives are formed by lengthening the final vowel of the casal form, so that they appear to have a plural form; for "first," the word is not derived from the numeral "one," but we have *rištānu,* lit. "the head one," for both genders, and *maḫru*, lit. "the foremost" or "front one," fem. *maḫritu*.

The others are:

2nd. *šanū*, fem.	*šanātu*.	*6th.* *šiššū* or *šišū*, f.	*šišātu*.
3rd. *šalšū*, ,,	*šalšātu*.	*7th.* *sibū*, ,,	*sibātu*.
4th. *ribū*, ,,	*ribātu*.	*8th.* *šamnū*, ,,	*šamnātu*.
5th. *ḫansū*, ,,	*ḫanšātu*.	*9th.* *tišū*, ,,	*tišātu*.
or *ḫaššū*, ,,	*ḫaššātu*.	*10th.* *esrū*, ,,	*ušrātu*, or *ešrātu*.

For the tens we have a similar formation: the 30th, *šelašū*.

Fractions.

The fractions are expressed by the cardinal numerals followed by the feminine of the ordinal:

šalsi ribāti, "three-fourths."

At a later period the masculine is found, III *ribi*, "three-fourths." Half is *mešlanu*, or *mešlu*.

The number 60 or the soss being taken as unit, the tens are used as the fractions of 60, and words used for these fractional numbers also used for the tens, as in Akkadian.

šinību, f. *šinipatu*, &c.

PERSONAL PRONOUNS.

The pronouns are the only part of the speech which has preserved flexions indicating the cases, like in the Aryan tongues.

Singular.

	1st Pers.	2nd Pers.	3rd Pers. Masc.	Fem.
Nom. . .	*anaku*,	*attakau*,	*šū*,	*šī*.
Gen. . .	*ia*,	*ka*,	*šu*,	*ši*.
Dat. and Abl.	*iāši*,	*kāši*,	*šuaši*,	*šiasi*.
Acc. . .	*iāti*,	*kāti*,	*šuati*,	*šiati*.

Plural.

	1st Pers.	2nd Pers.	3rd Pers. Masc.	Fem.
Nom. . .	*ninu* or *aninu*,	*attunu*,	*šunu*,	*šina*.
Gen. . .	*ni*,	*kunu*,	*šunu*,	*šina*.
Dat. and Abl.	*niaši* or *nāši*,	*kunuši*,	*šunuši*,	*šinaši*.
Acc. . .	*niati*,	*kunuti*,	*šunuti*,	*šinati*.

R. The form *attakau* was soon disused, and replaced by *atta* for the masculine, and *atti* for the feminine. In the genitive of the same person the genders are also distinguished: masc. *ka*, fem. *ki*.

The pronouns in the genitive being placed after the nouns in the construct state, are considered as possessive suffixes.

For the first person singular *ia* often becomes *ā*, *a*, or *i*, or is absorbed by the final vowel of the noun, *abi*, "my father."

For the second person singular, besides *ka*, we find *ḳu*, *ku*, and *ḳa*. These forms are used for the masculine. For the feminine *ki* is used.

For the third person feminine *ša* is also used, and at all the cases *ši* may become *si*.

The genitive forms used as suffixes may take a vowel of union, which is only a prolongation of the vowel of the noun, and the length may of course be represented by the doubling of the following consonant: *abūa*, "my father;" *kibitukka*, "thy will."

The final vowel of the genitive may be dropped: *ablus̆*, "his son;" *šarrikun*, "your king."

When the dative or ablative and accusative forms follow immediately the verb of which they are the indirect or direct objects, they may be considered as suffixes, and the initial consonant may be doubled.

The flexions of the pronouns are retained only in the earliest inscriptions; at the later period it is maintained only, and not always, for the third person plural.

As a rule, when the pronouns are direct or indirect objects of the verb, they are suffixed to the verb under a short form:

1st pers.	*-ni.*	plur. *-nini* or *-nu.*
2nd pers.	*-ka*, fem. *-ki.*	plur. *-kunu*, fem. *-kina.*
3rd pers.	*-šu*, fem. *-ši.*	plur. *-šunu*, fem. *-šina.*

The final vowel may be dropped, as for the possessive suffixes.

The Babylonians having forgotten the origin and notion of these flexions, assimilated the final vowel to the case-endings of the noun; so we find *kāšu, kāši,* and *kāša; šunutu, šunuti,* and *šunuta,* &c.

The plural formative in the pronoun, *-nu,* is sometimes added to the flexion: *šutunu, šitina, kāšunu,* &c., for *šunutu, šinati, kunuši.*

The mimation is also sometimes added to all the flexions: *iašim, kāšim, kašam, katim,* &c.

From the genitive *ia, ku,* &c., are formed possessive adjectives by adding *ū: iaū,* mine; *kaū,* thine.

An independent possessive adjective is formed by adding the suffixes to *atu* or *attu: abu, atūa,* or *attūa,* "my father;" but this is rare before the Persian period.

Demonstratives.

The personal pronoun of the third person is used as demonstrative adjective: *šū,* "this," fem. *šī.*

The accusative *šuati,* fem. *šiati,* was used for the nominative, and the final vowel assimilated to the case-endings; but the forms in *ti* were always used in preference even for the nominative.

By a similar assimilisation the dative form is used as a demonstrative: *šuasu, šuaši, šuaša,* fem. *šiašu,* &c.

We have also the relative combined with the possessive suffixes: *šāšu, šāši, šāsunu, šāšina.*

The other demonstratives are:

ammu,	fem.	*ammatu,*	plur.	*ammūtu,*	fem.	*ammātu.*
annu,	,,	*annitu,*	,,	*annūtu,*	,,	*annātu.*
ullu,	,,	*ullatu,*	,,	*ullutu,*	,,	*ullātu.*

These three pronouns, instead of the plural in *ūtu*, can also take another plural in *ē*: *ammē, annē, ullē.*

There is another demonstrative of doubtful origin:

aga, agā, or *agaʿ*, fem. *agata*, plur. *aganutu*, fem. *aganātu.*

It may be combined with the personal pronoun, *agašū* or *šūaga*, &c., also with the demonstrative *annu.*

Relative.

There is only one relative, which is invariable: *ša*, "who, whom, which," &c.

Interrogative.

The interrogatives are *mi*, "who, why;" *man, manu*, "who;" *manume*, "who."

The Indefinite Pronouns are:

mamma, manma, manamma, } "anything,"
mimmu, plur. *mimmemi* or *mimemi,* } "everything."
iaumma, "whatever."
šanamma, "another."
mala, "everything."

For the negative, *la* is simply put before.

For "one another," *aḥames* is used, but for "some . . . others," we find also *anute . . . anute, aḥadi . . . aḥadi*, &c.

VERB.

The verb has four principal voices, having each a secondary and a tertiary form or voice.

The first voice, or Kal, is the stem simple without addition.

The second, or Niphal, is formed by prefixing *na* to the stem.

The third, or Shaphel, is formed by prefixing *ša* to the stem.

The fourth, or Pael, is formed by doubling the middle radical of the stem.

The secondary voices are formed by the insertion of *ta* after the first syllable of the principal or primary voices.

The tertiary voices are formed by inserting *tan* or *tana* in the same way.

Moods and Tenses.

The Assyro-Babylonian verb is rich in forms. There are nine moods, including the infinitive, which is, however, not a mood of the verb, but which, properly speaking, is composed of nominal and adjectival forms, as will be seen farther on.

The moods and tenses may be classified thus:

1. *Infinitive:* simple, participle present, participle continuous, participle past-active, and participle past-passive.
2. *Indicative:* aorist, mutative, precative.
3. *Imperative:* aorist, mutative.
4. *Permensive:* simple, precative.
5. *Subjective:* aorist, mutative, precative.
6. *Dependent:* ,, ,, ,,
7. *Objective:* ,, ,, ,,
8. *Energetic:* ,, ,, ,,
9. *Paragogic:* ,, ,, ,,

Formation of Tenses.

INFINITIVE.

In the Assyro-Babylonian language, as it is known to us, all the words were considered, by those who spoke and wrote it, as derived from a theme or root formed of three letters, generally consonants, and called radicals: XYZ. These themes represented to the mind an abstract notion or idea, and to give to them life, so to say, vowels were to be added.

The words so formed from the abstract themes do not, properly speaking, form part of the verb, and they are generally considered as nouns or adjectives; but as it is from them that the various tenses are formed, they must be mentioned.

All the verbal forms may be brought back to five nominal formations, obtained from the theme by different vocalisations.

(1.) *Infinitive simple.—XaYāZ* gives the abstract notion of the theme, and answers exactly to our infinitive, no account being taken of time or duration: *šakānu*, "to place;" *raḫāṣu*, "to inundate;" *zakāru*, "to record;" *ḫabātu*, "to plunder;" *rakāsu*, "to bind;" *makāsu*, "to impose (a tax);" *rakābu*, "to ride;" *balātu*, "to live;" *šatāru*, "to write," &c.

All these words are really abstract nouns of action or state, and might therefore be translated: a placing, inundation, a recording, &c. But the close connection of these words with the real verbs was always preserved in the mind of the Babylonians, and they were used exactly like our infinitives.

(2.) *Participle present.—XaYiZ* forms nouns of agents, and answers exactly to our present participle. It gives the notion of the action being done for the time being: *šakin*, "placing;" *raḫiṣ*, "inundating, a shower;" *zakir*, "recording, recorder;" *rakiš*, "binding;" *rakibu*, "riding, a charioteer;" *makis*, "taxing, a taxer," &c.

(3.) *Participle continuous.—XaYaZ* expresses the action being done and lasting, and answers more exactly to our names of agents. The examples of this form, as of the following, are less numerous, as their use was subjected in a great extent to the caprice of the nominal formation and of the custom of the speakers: *šakan*, subj. *šaknu*, "the placer *or* doer, *i.e.*, governor;" *zakar*, subj. *zakru*, "the one who records," taken as adjective, "mentioned," because the thing mentioned, which has a name, is a perpetual recorder; *rakab*, subj. *rakabu* or *rakbu*, "ambassador," because he is constantly riding or travelling; *šaṭaru*, "inscription, writing," because the inscription keeps permanently the writing, is being inscribed; also used as adjective, "inscribed," &c.

(4.) *Participle past-active.—XiYiZ* indicates the result of the action completed; it answers to a great extent to our nouns, like "rain," the result of "raining;" "deed," result of "doing;" "a run," the space run through, &c.: *šikin*, subj. *šiknu*, "the space," from the meaning "to do;" *riḫiṣ*, subj. *riḫṣu*, with the fem. form *riḫiṣtu*, "inundation," or "a shower" after it is over; *zikir*, "name," result of recording; *šiṭir*, subj. *šiṭiru*, "a writing," the body of the contract, result of "writing;" *šibib*, subj. *šibbu*, "crown," result of the action of "bending round" (*šabābu*), &c.

(5.) *Participle past-passive.—XuYuZ* expresses the result of the action as suffered by the object, and answers to our past-participle: *šukun*, in the fem. *šukuttu* (for *šukuntu*), "tool," what has been done; *ḫubut*, subj. *ḫubtu*, "booty," what has been plundered; *buluṭ*, subj. *bulṭu*, "alive," as a noun "the living," what has received life; *rukub*, subj. *rukubu*, "a chariot," what is ridden, also "the course," the ground which is ridden on, &c.

The two last formations have been often confused, and the same theme appears in the two forms with the same meaning, as *šikittu* (for *šikintu*) and *šukuttu* (for *šukuntu*), "tool;" or the same form has the meanings of the active and passive, as from *rakāsu*, "to bind;" *rikis*, subj. *riksu*, "a contract," the result of "binding," and "the waist," the part which is bound (cf. French *ceinture*).

All these forms, being in reality nouns or adjectives, follow the same rules as to the formation of the feminine and plural, and as to the case-endings.

When the theme has two radicals the same letter, one of them is often doubled: *šulullu* by the side of *šullu* (subj. of *šulul*), participle past-passive of *šalālu*, "to carry away."

Infinitives of the other voices are very rarely found in the texts, and appear only as nouns or adjectives.

The infinitives, as given by modern Assyriologists, are in all the voices formed from the participle past-passive, to which is added the formative prefixes of the various voices. For the theme *škn* the twelve infinitives restored by analogy are:[1]

[1] In the excellent paper of Mr. Pincher on the Permensive, the nomenclature of the Hebrew grammar is preserved, Kal, Niphal, &c., because it has the advantage to be understood.

Kal, *šakānu.*	K², *šitakunu.*	K³, *šitankunu.*
Niphal, *naškunu.*	N², *itaškunu.*	N³, *itanaškunu.*
Shaphel, *šuškunu.*	S², *šutaškunu.*	S³, *šutanaskunu.*
Pael, *šukkunu.*	P², *šitakkunu.*	P³, *šitanakkunu.*

These infinitives are real nouns, and follow the same rules as the nouns for the formation of the feminine and plural, &c.

The secondary and tertiary voices of the Niphal show the weakening and the total loss of the characteristic *n*: *itaskunu* and *itanaškunu* is for *nitaskunu* and *nitanaškunu.*

It is to be noticed that all these forms are passive, and really participles past-passive of the same type as in the Kal *XuYuZ.* It is, therefore, not correct to call them infinitives simple.

A few forms accidentally found show besides that real infinitives simple, corresponding to the Kal form *XaYāZu*, existed in the language, but those found are considered as nouns or adjectives, like the Niphal *napṭāru*, "to defend," and the Shaphel *šapšāḳu*, "steep."

These forms were considered as the real infinitives or *nomina verbi* by the Babylonians, and are those given in the syllabaries.

The infinitives of the secondary voices have always *i* before the inserted *t*, as in *gitmalu*, "benefactor," from *gamālu*, "to spare."

The infinitives of the tertiary voices have not been found.

The forms of the infinitive simple may be restored, for the stem BLT (life, to give life, to live, &c.), thus:

Kal, *balāṭu.*	K², *bitlāṭu.*	K³, *bitanlaṭu.*
Niphal, *nablāṭu.*	N², *(n)itablāṭu.*	N³, *(n)itanablaṭu.*
Shaphel, *šablātu.*	S², *šitablāṭu.*	S³, *šitanablaṭu.*
Pael, *ballātu.*	P², *bitallāṭu.*	P³, *batanallaṭu.*

Examples of the participles present are found only in nouns and adjectives like *naḫliptu*, feminine form of the participle present Niphal of *halāpu*, "to cover."

The examples of the participle continuous are not so scarce. For the Niphal we have *namraṣu*, "impassable," from *marāṣu*, "to be unwell;" for the Pael, *rakkabu*, "a chariot;" but these forms must have been easily confounded with those of the true infinitive simple.

The participle past-active was naturally very rare in those voices having a tendency to be considered as passive. Only the Pael, *kiṣṣillu*, "royal," from *kaṣālu*, may be quoted, and has the last radical doubled as well as the second.

The past-participle passive has been more preserved, and forms regularly the permensive of all these voices; the restored forms have been given above, because it is the ones generally given as the infinitive by Assyriologists.

The words formed with these participles were no doubt avoided on account of their length, and examples are not so rare with the weak stems.

All these voices have also a compound participle formed by the prefix *mu* added to the other participle. It is found with the Kal forms, but in the other voices it is more regularly used:

> *muntaḥṣu* (constr. *muntaḥiṣ*), "soldier," from the Niphal of *taḥāṣu*, "to fight."
> *munnakalu*, "concealed," from the Niphal of *nakālu*, "to build."

In the Shaphel the vowel following the *š* is either *a* or *e*:

> *mušakniš* and *mušekniš*, from *kanāšu*, "to subject."

In the Pael the double letter of the middle radical is often written simple:

> *munakkir*, "destroyer," from *nakāru*, *mumaḥir*, "director," from *maḥāru*.

The secondary and tertiary voices are regularly formed from the participles of the Kal:

> *mukṭabil*, subj. *muktablu*, "fighter, one who places himself in the middle (of the battle)," from *kabālu*, "to be in the middle."

These compound participles may be formed from all the participles of Kal, but are generally considered as nominal or adjectival formations:

munirriṭu, "struggling," from the Pael of *narāṭu*.

Indicative or Construct Mood.

AORIST.

The aorist is formed by means of prefixes added to one of the participles; the genders and numbers are distinguished by the vowel suffixed to the form.

Sing. 1st pers. com. *a—*	2nd pers.	masc. *ta—*	3rd pers.	masc. *i—*
		fem. *ta—i*		fem. *ta—*
Plur. " " *ni—*	"	masc. *ta—u*	"	masc. *i—u*
		fem. *ta—a*		fem. *i—a*

When these prefixes are added to the participles, the first vowel of this is almost invariably dropped; we have, therefore:

From the participle continuous:	1st pers.	*aXYaZ*,	2nd pers.	*taXYaZ*, &c.
From the participle past-active:	"	*aXYiZ*,	"	*taXYiZ*, &c.
From the participle past-passive:	"	*aXYuZ*,	"	*taXYuZ*, &c.

When the aorist is derived from the participle present, what is exceedingly rare, the vowel of the first radical is preserved, unless it would be confounded with a form derived from the participle past-active, and it is 1st pers. *aXaYiZ*, 2nd pers. *taXaYiZ*, &c.

The prefixes given above, which form the various persons, are the remnants of auxiliary verbs; if their auxiliary character is not lost sight of, the formation of the aorist appears quite consistent and rational. For instance, *aškun*, "I placed," from *šakānu*, "to place," is a form exactly parallel to "I have placed," formed from the auxiliary *a* and the past-participle passive, *šukun*. In the same way:

amšuḥ = "I have measured," from *mašāḥu*, "to measure."
taškun = "thou hast placed," from *šakānu*, "to place."
nišṭur = "we have written," from *šaṭāru*, "to write."

And these forms may be explained more correctly thus:

aškun, "I have (the thing) placed;" *amšuḥ*, "I have (the thing) measured," &c.

With the participle continuous the form may be analysed in the same way:

iṣbat = "he has a taking," from *ṣabatu*, "to take."

But there is a difference in meaning corresponding to that attached to the participle used as formative:

iṣbat is "he has a taking of a thing, and retains possession of it."

With the participle past-active:

abšil = "I have a cooking (a stew)," from *bašālu*, "to cook," which really is "I have the thing which was once cooked (as a stew, a piece of roast-beef, &c.)."

Originally no doubt every verb could form its aorist from all the participles indifferently, and had in reality four aorists; but in practice only one was retained, and it is only accidentally that the same stem is found to have several forms for the aorist, as:

iṣbat and *iṣbut*, "he took."

The notion of the auxiliary character of the prefixes was lost, and at the same time also the origin of the formation forgotten. The verbal forms were then considered as uncompound, and to distinguish the genders and numbers a vowel was suffixed—*i* for the feminine singular, and in the plural *u* for the masculine, *a* for the feminine, and for the dual *ā*.

The greatest number of the verbs retained exclusively the aorist (in *u*) formed from the participle past-passive, as the following:

ḥabātu, "to plunder;" *ḥamātu*, "to hasten;" *ḥasāḥu*, "to desire;" *gamāru*, "to be complete;" *kabāšu*, "to trample upon;" *kanāku*, "to seal;" *karābu*, "to be propitious;" *ḳapādu*, "to level;" *kaṣāru*, "to run away;" *babālu*, "to pull down;" *batāku*, "to detach;" *paṭāru*, "to free;" *paḫaru*, "to collect;" *parasu*, "to destroy;" *magāru*, "to obey;" *maḳātu*, "to fall;" *mašāḫu*, "to measure;" *šadādu*, "to drag;" *ragāmu*, "to ask;" *rakāsu*, "to bind;" *ramāku*, "to pour out;" *radādu*, "to pursue;" *šalālu*, "to carry away;" *šarāpu*, "to burn;" *šaṭāru*, "to write;" *šaḫāpu*, "to overwhelm;" *zakāru*, "to record;" *šahāpu*, "to sweep away;" *ṣarāpu*, "to melt;" *dabāku*, "to spread;" *darāku*, "to be cast down;" *ṭarādu*, "to drive away;" *takāpu*, "to take hold;" *tabāku*, "to pour out;" *tamāḫu*, "to grasp;" and many others.

A small number has retained the exclusive use of the aorist (in *i*) formed from the participle past-active, as the following:

ḫapāru, "to bring out;" *ḫalāḳu*, "to injure;" *gašāru*, "to strengthen;" *bašālu*, "to cook;" *bašāmu*, "to dispose;" *patāḫu*, "to build;" *parāru*, "to disperse;" *rašāpu*, "to build;" *raṣāpu*, "to join;" *labānu*, "to cast down;" *šalāmu*, "to pacify;" *šazānu*, "to be angry;" *ṣakābu*, "to overthrow;" *dagālu*, "to see;" and a few others.

A few verbs have exclusively the aorist (in *a*) formed with the participle continuous, as the following:

parāku, "to divide;" *patāḫu*, "to fear;" *maḫāṣu*, "to fight;" *šanānu*, "to be equal;" *takālu*, "to trust," &c.

As said above, in a few cases verbs have preserved the use of two aorists, though the same meaning is attached to both: *ḳarābu*, "to collect," has the two forms *iḳrub* and *iḳrib; ṣabātu*, "to take," *iṣbat* and *iṣbut*, *maḫāru*, "to receive," *imḫur* and *imḫar*, &c.

As for the aorist derived from the participle present, it must be acknowledged that its very existence is doubtful, for such forms as *ipašiṭu*, "they destroyed," from *pašāṭu*, "to destroy," may be mutatives, in which the second or middle radical has not been doubled, as it often happens (see farther on), and used for aorists.

In the other voices the aorist is derived from the participle present, rarely from the participle past-active.

The prefixes indicating the persons remain the same in the secondary and tertiary voice of Kal and in Niphal and its two voices, but for the other voices the vowel of these prefixes is *u* in all the persons, thus:

Singular.

1st Pers.	2nd Pers. Masc.	Fem.	3rd Pers. Masc.	Fem.
u—	*tu—*	*tu—i*	*u—*	*tu—*

Plural.

1st Pers.	2nd Pers. Masc.	Fem.	3rd Pers. Masc.	Fem.
nu—	*tu—u*	*tu—a*	*u—u*	*u—a*

In the Niphal the characteristic *n* is generally assimilated: *ikkibus* (for *inkibus*), "he was conquered," from *kabāsu*.

In the Shaphel the vowel following the *š* characteristic may be *a*, *e*, or *i*:

ušakniš, *ušekniš*, and *ušikniš*, from *kanāšu*, "to submit."
ušaḫlika, from *ḫalāku*, "to destroy."
ušiklil, from *kalālu*, "to end."

In the Pael the doubling of the middle radical is often neglected:

uballik, "I divided," from *balaku*.
tukattiri, "thou hast surrounded," from *katāru*.
uzakkir and *uzakir*, "I completed," from *zakāru*.

In the secondary voices the vowel of the characteristic letter *t* may be *a*, *e*, or *i*:

iḫtalik, from *ḫalāku*, "to destroy."
iḫteṣin, from *ḫaṣanu*.
uštaḳṣir, from *ḳaṣāru*.
uptaššit, from *pašātu*.
aḳtirib, from *ḳarābu*.

For the tertiary voices the aorist is regularly formed from the participle past active or passive.

iḳdanaludu K^3 from *kalādu*.
ittanabrik N^3 from *barāku*.

MUTATIVE.

The mutative is formed with the same prefixes as the aorist added to the participle present or the participle continuous, but the middle radical of these participles is doubled in order to either strengthen the idea conveyed to the mind by the verbal noun, or, most probably, because the action is actually performed by the subject. The origin of this tense is the same, in fact, as that of the Pael, having the force of a passive, or rather middle voice, as it is called in Greek. This explanation is supported by the fact that in great many cases the mutative of the Kal is replaced by the mutative of the Pael (see SYNTAX). The mutative may therefore be explained in the same way as the aorist, but the auxiliary is to be translated by the verb "to be":

arakkis = "I am binding," from *rakāsu*, "to bind."
inadin = "he is giving," from *nadānu*, "to give."
tašakkin = "thou art placing," from *šakānu*, "to place."

When derived from the participle continuous, the mutative had naturally a slight difference in meaning:

ašakkan = "I am placer," from *šakānu*, "to place."
inaddan = "he is giver," from *nadanu*, "to give."
iḫassas = "he is sinner," from *ḫasāsu*, "to sin."
taṣabbat = "thou art taker," from *ṣabātu*, "to take."

From the origin of these two forms it appears quite rational that they should have been used to express the present or the future. The first is more properly the present, for it indicates the subject of the verb as being in the act of performing the action, and the second is a continuous present or future. In practice, however, the two forms were confounded, and most of the verbs have retained only one.

As noticed in the phonology, a double consonant was often written simple; the mutative in this case is distinguished from the aorist only by its vocalisation and the presence of a vowel after the first radical. We have:

iškun, "he placed;" *išakan*, "he places" or "shall place."
izkur, "he recorded;" *izakar*, "he records" or "shall record."
indin, "he gave;" *inadin*, "he gives" or "shall give."
imḫar, "he received;" *imaḫar*, "he receives" or "shall receive."

Sometimes we find abnormal vocalisations, as *iraggum*, "he disputes," from *ragāmu*, but it is no doubt due to the fact that in these cases the mutative has been derived from a nominal form not noticed above.

For all the other voices, the mutative is formed from the participle continuous with the same prefixes as in the aorist of the same voice:

iššakan (for *inšakan*), N., from *šakānu*.
attakil and *atakil* (for *antakil*), N., from *takālu*.
ušaḫnap, S., from *ḫanāpu*.
usaḫḫar, P., from *saḫāru*.
upaḫar, P., from *pahāru*.
aštakan, K^2, from *šakānu*.
ittaškan, N^2, from *šakānu*.
uštaklal, S^2, from *kalālu*.
ittanagrar, N^3, from *garāru*.

Precative.

The precative is formed for all the voices by the particle *lu*, "be it," prefixed to the verbal forms of the aorist or mutative. There are therefore two precatives, but in practice only one of them has been, as a rule, preserved with the same meaning of simple precative, though primitively there must have been a slight shade of meaning between them.

When the verbal form begins with *a*, this letter is dropped or assimilated to the *u* of the prefix: *lūbluṭ*, "may I live," from *balātu*.

When the verbal form begins with *i*, the vowel *u* of the prefix is dropped or assimilated: *liḫlik* and *liḫallik*, from *ḫalāku*; *liškun*, from *šakānu*.

Imperative.

Aorist.—The aorist has only one person, the second of the singular and plural. It is formed from one of the participles; the great majority of the verbs form it from the past-participle passive (*XuYuZ*), a small number from the past-participle active (*XiYiZ*), and a few from the participle continuous (*XaYaZ*), and fewer still from the participle present (*XaYiZ*). The same verb might take two different forms. Probably at the origin the aorist of the imperative was formed indifferently from the various participles, according to the idea which the speaker wanted to convey, the imperative being, in fact, nothing else than the stem. When it took the vocalisation of one of the participles, it also took the idea attached to it. In practice, however, one form only survived for each verb, and it follows that adopted for the aorist of the indicative:

iškun, "he placed;" *šukun*, "place thou."
iprus, "he freed;" *purus*, "free thou."

The feminine is distinguished from the masculine in the singular by an addition of the vowel *i*, and the plural takes *u* for the masculine and *a* for the feminine; but in these cases the second vowel (that placed after the second radical) is generally dropped: *šukna*, "place ye."

Mutative.—The mutative of the imperative is formed in the same way as the aorist, and as for the mutative of the indicative by the doubling of the second radical, from the participle present or the participle continuous. It has only one person (the second), the genders and numbers being distinguished in the same way as for the aorist. The two forms (*XaYYiZ* and *XaYYaZ*) might be found with the same stem, but the form preserved generally follows the same formation as the mutative of the indicative. The use of this tense being very rare, the examples are very scarce.

In the other voices the imperative follows also the indicative in its formation in some cases, but, as a rule, it is derived from a special form, *XuYiZ*. The vowel following the *n* of the

Niphal is *a*, but that following the *š* of the Shaphel is *u*. In the secondary voices the vowel preceding the *t* characteristic is always *i*.

Permensive.

The permensive is formed from the participle present for the Kal, with a few exceptions, and from the participle past-passive for all the other voices. This tense is, properly speaking, nothing else than a participle; in the third person the subject being generally expressed by a noun or an emphatic pronoun, the participle is used without addition, but the other persons are distinguished by suffixes added to the participle, in the subjective or objective case, its final vowel being elided, it is difficult to say why. The suffixes are:

Sing. 1st pers. *-aku* or *-ak;* 2nd, *-āta*.
Plur. „ *-āni* or *-ānu;* „ *-ātunu*.

The genders are not distinguished in the 1st and 2nd persons.

Sing. 1st pers. *raḫṣak*, "I am trusting, or one who trusts," from *rahāṣu;*
taklak, "I am protecting, or one who protects," from *takāla*.
2nd masc. *šaknata*, "thou art establishing," from *šakānu*.
3rd masc. *šakin*, "he is establishing or making," from *šakānu*.
Plur. 1st pers. *balṭānu*, "we are living," from *balāṭu*.
3rd masc. *ṣabtu* or *ṣabtuni*, "they are taking," from *ṣabātu*.
„ fem. *saḫrā*, "they are surrounding," from *saḫāra*.

In a very few verbs the permensive Kal seems to be formed from the participle past active or passive, more often from the latter, and as a rule this is found with verbs denoting a state.

3rd pers. *lumun* or *limun*, "he is evil," fem. *limnit;* 2nd pers. plural, *limnitunu*, "you are evil," from *lamānu*, "to be evil."

It is seen by the last example that the connecting vowel is harmonised:

mašālu, "to be like," makes *mašil* and *mušul*.
marāṣu, "to be ill," makes *maruṣ*; *mariṣ* is also found.

The permensive appears to have been formed originally with all the participles, and could be formed even with nouns and adjectives, like, for instance, *šarraku*, "I am king."

For the other voices:

N. 3rd pers. *našmur*, "he holds *or* watches," from *šamāru*.
S. „ *šuklul*, "he has caused to complete," from *kalālu*.
P. „ *dulluḫu*, "he was troubled," from *dalaḫu*.
K². „ (fem.) *šitkunat*, "she was situated," from *šakānu*.
N². „ *itamgur* (for *nitamgur*), "he obeys," from *magāru*.
S². „ *šutasḫur*, "he cause to enclose," from *saḫāru*.
P². „ not found.

The tertiary voices are not found.

A precative could be formed from the permensive by prefixing the affix *lū* to all the forms.

Subjective Mood.

All the tenses of the subjective mood are formed from the corresponding ones of the indicative by adding *u* to the forms of the indicative in the singular: ind. aorist, *iškun*; subj. aorist, *iškunu*; and *nu* or *ni* in the plural:

ikpuduni, from *kapādu*, "to cover."
liḳrubuni, from *ḳarābu*, "to collect."

Dependent Mood.

All the tenses of the dependent mood are formed in the same way by adding *i* for the singular, and *uni* for the plural:

Indicative, *iškun*. Dependent, *iškuni*.
„ *iṣbatu* „ *iṣbatuni*.

Objective Mood.

All the tenses of the objective are formed in the same way by adding *a* for the singular:

Indicative, *iškun.*	Objective, *iškuna.*
„ *taṣbat.*	„ *taṣbata.*

Energetic Mood.

This mood includes all the verbal forms having the mimation; but this mood is rare, it being confounded with the following. From this fact it may be inferred that the doubling of the *m* only indicates the length of the preceding vowel, or is written only to prevent the weakening and dropping of the characteristic *m*.

Paragagic Mood.

Under this name we class all the forms having the mimation followed by the enclitic *ma*:

akbasumma, from *kabāsu*.
ittaḥlibamma, from N^2 of *ḥalābu*.
ipšilunimma, from *pašālu*.

WEAK VERBS.

All the apparent irregularities of the weak verbs, that is, the verbs having an *n*, the aspirate ', or a vowel as one of their radicals, are easily explained by the phonetic laws of the language.

For instance, a verb having *n* for first radical, like *našāku*, is to a certain extent treated as Niphal of a supposed *šaku*, and makes its infinitive of the secondary Kal voice in *itašuku*. When the *n* comes into contact with the second radical, it is assimilated, and then considered as only indicating the existence of a long vowel; hence the verb falls into the category of those having a vowel as first radical.

The length of a syllable being often represented by the doubling of the next consonant, we have therefore *illik*, "he went," for *īlik* from *ālāku*.

In the Niphal the length of the vowel of these verbs is often represented by the *n* following it, and we have for the infinitive, *nanluku*, from *ālāku*, *nenpusu*, from *ēpešu*, "to do," &c., and in the aorist 3rd pers. sing. *innalik*, *innepiš*, &c.

The verbs having ' or *ū* for first radical are treated as those having *ā*, those having *ī* as those having *ē*. The personal prefixes remain the same in the first case, the vowel being only lengthened. In the second case the vocalisation is *ē* or *ī* for all persons. Some verbs having primitively *u* as first radical preserve it, and this *u* absorbs the vowel of the prefixes; so the prefixes of the persons are the same as for the Pael: *ulid*, "I bore (a son)," for (*aulid*), from (*u*)*alādu*.

For the verbs weak of the second radical the vowels of the first and second radicals are generally contracted into one, but sometimes there are attempts to represent them; in this case we may suppose the presence of an aspirate unwritten: *kain* (for *ka'in*) by the side of *kin*, third person permensive of *kānu*.

It is to be noticed that the different kinds of weak verbs are often confounded; we find *attur* by the side of *atur* (for *atūr*), 1st. pers. aorist of *tāru*.

The verbs weak of the last radical preserve their final vowel in all the tenses, but it is generally the same for the aorist or the mutative: *ḳabū*, "to speak," makes aorist *aḳbi*, mutative *aḳabbi*.

It is to be noticed that there was always a tendency to strengthen the weaḳ verbs, and the secondary and tertiary voices are, for this reason, no doubt, of a more frequent use with the weak verbs.

Quadrilitary and Quinquilitary Stems.

The stems having four or five consonants as radicals are treated as derivative voices, even if the radicals which form the first part of them are not those used to form derivatives.

PREPOSITIONS.

There are only a few real prepositions: *ana*, "to, in;" *ina*, "in, from, with;" *ultu* or *ištu*, "from;" *adi*, "till, to;" *ki* or *kima*, "as."

The other prepositions are really nouns, and may take the possessive suffixes: *itti*, "with;" from *ittu*, "place;" *itti-ka*, "with thee" or "thy place;" *eli*, "over;" *arki*, "after, behind;" *pani*, "before, in front of;" *maḫri*, "in front of," &c.

The feminine form of the same nouns which form these prepositions can be used in the same way: *arkat*, *maḫrit*, &c.

It is generally the construct case which is used.

ADVERBS.

The adverbs of manner can be derived from all nouns by adding *š* to the dependent case: *rabi*, "great," *rabiš*; *libbi*, "heart," *libbiš*, "cordially;" *edi*, "one," *edis*, "alone;" *eli*, "high," *eliš*, "above;" *kakkabi*, "star," *kakkabiš*, "as a star" or "starlike."

Nouns in any form can be used adverbially (see Syntax).

Adverbial expressions are formed by prepositions: *ina umū annute*, "in these days;" *ultu ulla*, "from old."

Adverbs are formed by the enclitic *ma*: *umma*, "thus;" *matema*, "in times past;" *kalama*, "of all sorts;" *panama*, "formerly;" *kiaam*, "thus," &c.

The negatives are: *la*, *ul* (before a verb), *ā* (before a verb or in composition), *aumma*, "never."

CONJUNCTIONS.

The principal conjunctions are: *u* or *ū*, "and," sometimes "or;" *lū*, "or;" *ma* (enclitic), "and, so that, in order that;" *kī*, "if, when, as, while;" *aššu* or *aššum*, "when, as for;" *šumma*, "if, when;" *ni* (enclitic), "so."

The relative *ša* is also used as a conjunction, "that, because," &c., and forms compound conjunctions with the prepositions: *adi ša*, "in so far as;" *adi eli ša*, "till;" *arki ša*, "after that," exactly like "that" in English and *que* in French.

Some conjunctions are also formed with nouns followed by *ša*: *libbu ša*, "just as."

SYNTAX.

Nouns.

In the earliest inscriptions and documents (age of Hammurabi) the three cases terminate with the mimation; at the other periods it is only preserved, and not always with feminine or abstract nouns in *t* and a few others. In the syllabaries and word-lists the mimation is generally given as the regular and proper ending, but in poetry the mimation is also often neglected.

At a later period the mimation or the emphatic state are used, very much as our article: *kaspam* or *kaspa'*, "the money (which has been mentioned before)."

When a noun is followed by another which depends upon it, or by the possessive suffixes, it cannot take the mimation or the emphatic state.

The subjective case is used when the noun is the subject. The dependent case is used when the word is governed by another noun, *i.e.*, in the genitive or after a preposition. The objective case is used when the word is the object of the verb, *i.e.*, in the accusative. The construct state is used when the word governs another noun, which is then in the dependent case. The possessive suffixes are sometimes added to the construct state.

We find compound words formed with two nouns, one in the construct state and the other in the dependent case: *bel ekli*, "landlord," lit. "lord of the field."

When the genitive is expressed emphatically by means of the relative *ša*, the regent takes the case-ending: *belu ša ekli*, "the lord of the field," lit. "the lord who (is) of the field."

The nouns with possessive suffixes are sometimes put in the construct state even when not followed by a genitive.

The plural in *ū* appears more often under the form *e—ile* for *ilū*, "the gods,"—or even in *i*, *ilī*.

The construct state of the plural in *anu* is hardly ever found; the form in *ani* is used for all cases.

The abstract nouns in *ūtu* or *uttu* may be used as singular nouns: *ameluttu*, "the slave" or "the slaves." Other nouns are taken collectively: *nišu*, "men" or "people."

Certain words are used more often in the plural: *me* for *mue*, "water," by the side of *mu*.

When two nouns are placed in apposition, the second is treated as an adjective, and agrees with the first in number, gender, and case.

With numbers, names of measures, weights, &c., are put in the dependent case of the singular: xv *gurri*, "fifteen tons," lit. "fifteen of ton."

When a noun is used as explicative complement, explaining or emphasising the meaning of the verb, it may be in the subjective, objective, or dependent case, or in the construct state.

Except in a very few cases, and especially in poetry, the adjective follows the noun it qualifies and agrees with it in number, gender, and case.

When the noun is in the construct state (or in the dependent case), with a possessive suffix, the following adjective is put in the normal case which the noun would take if it had no suffix.

The participles may govern the dependent case, but the noun governed by it may also be put in the objective case, and then may precede it.

In a few cases adjectives are treated in the same way.

The comparative and superlative of comparation are expressed by the adjective followed by a preposition: *rabu ina ilani*, "the greatest of the gods," lit. "the great among the gods."

The superlative of abstraction is sometimes expressed by a reduplicate form of the adjective: *dandannu*, "very strong."

The comparative and superlative are also expressed by the adjective followed by the relative: *rabu ša ilani*, lit. "the great of the gods."

NUMERALS.

The cardinal numerals are treated as abstracts, and therefore placed before the nouns: *ešten ameluttu*, "one slave" or "one of a slave."

In practice the masculine forms of the cardinals from 3 to 10 were used with feminine nouns, and the feminine forms with the masculine nouns. Sometimes the numeral agrees with the noun and follows, it being treated as an adjective. These rules are not, however, always adhered to.

The cardinals treated as abstracts may be followed by the noun in the dependent case of the singular.

The ordinals are real adjectives and follow the same rules.

In the Babylonian contracts the month is given first, and is followed by the day, then the year and the name of the king, thus: *arḫu adaru, umu šalšū, šattu ešrū, Nabu-naʿid šar Babili*, "month Adar, day third, year tenth, Nabonidus, king of Babylon."

Sometimes the cardinals are, as in French, used for the ordinals, and in this case generally placed before the nouns.

PRONOUNS.

The personal pronouns in the nominative, when used emphatically, are placed before the verb, and generally at the beginning of the sentence.

When the verb substantive is understood, the pronoun is generally thrown to the end of the sentence, taking thus the place of the verb.

The use of the two oblique flexional cases are regularly observed only in the documents of the time of Hammurabi and in a few old poetic texts. In the others, the pronominal suffixes are used in the same form with the verb to express the dative and accusative: *iddin-šunuti*, "he gave them or to them."

At all periods the flexional dative in *āši* (*āšu*, *āša*) is used also to express the ablative: *kāši*, "to, by, or from thee;" and after a preposition: *ana kāši*, "to thee."

After a preposition the accusative is also used: *ana iāti*, "to me."

The dative is sometimes used to express the genitive case.

The plural of the second person is used in the nominative, *attunu*, as dative and accusative, and even as a suffix attached to the verb.

The accusative is used for the vocative case.

The pronouns with the suffix of the accusative (*iati*, *kāti*, &c.) are used as subject of a secondary clause of a complex sentence (see SYNTAX OF SENTENCES).

The pronominal possessive adjectives may be used independently or as the possessive suffixes after a noun. In the first case they precede the noun, which is considered as being in apposition: *iaū abil libbīa*, "the son of my heart," lit. "mine, the son of my heart."

Sometimes these possessive adjectives imply the verb substantive; they are then thrown to the end of the sentence, and may take the enclitic *ma* or a lengthening *m* vocalised by harmony: *kummu*, "it is thine" or "they are thine."

In the same way the personal pronouns can take the enclitic

ma with the same force: *attama*, "thou art" or "it is thou;" *iatima*, "it is I."

The pronominal suffixes are used to denote the direct or indirect object: *iddin-šu* is "he gave him" or "he gave to him." When the two objects are expressed, or when the writer wishes to avoid ambiguity, the pronominal suffix representing the indirect object is preceded by a preposition or another turn is used: *ina ḳati-šu iddin*, "he gave into his hand."

The suffixes are added sometimes emphatically to the verbs when the words they represent are already expressed, even if the object is an emphatic pronoun with the flexion: *kāša luḳbi-ka*, "may I relate to thee."

The possessive suffix of the third person masculine, *šu*, is used for the feminine in the dialect of Babylon.

The third person pronoun is used with an indeterminate meaning representing "some one" or "some of them" understood.

Relative Pronoun.

There is only one relative pronoun, *ša*, for all genders, numbers, and cases. The oblique cases and other relations are expressed by means of the possessive suffix added to the regent: *ša abi-šu*, "whose father," lit. "who his father;" *ša ina eli-šu*, "over whom," lit. "who over him." In the same way *abli-šu ša*, "son of," lit. "son of he who (is)."

Sometimes the relative is followed by the noun or expression it represents placed in apposition: *ša Cambuzīa aḫu-šu*, "whose (Cambyses') brother," lit. "who, Cambyses his brother."

Demonstratives.

The pronouns of the third person are used as demonstratives: *amelu šū*, "this man;" *aššatu šī*, "this woman;" they always follow the noun, but are not to be considered as suffixes: *šelalti šunu*, "these three."

The accusative form has come to be used for the nominative: *bitu šuati*, "this house."

The same anomalies are noticed for the other demonstratives.

VERBS.

The third person masculine in the singular is generally used for the feminine, and the feminine for the masculine in the plural. In the other cases the verb agrees with its subject in number and gender.

When two subjects are united by the copula *u*, the verb agrees with the first.

The verb is put in the plural with a singular subject when it is considered as a collective noun.

Verbs can have only one direct object; when there are two, the second must be considered either as a noun in apposition or as the name of manner explaining the action of the verb; in the latter case it is really a noun or expression taken adverbially. Sometimes this explanatory noun is preceded by *ana* or *kima*, or takes the adverbial form in *iš*. When there is no preposition before it, it may be in the construct state or have the casal form, according to the view taken by the writer. When in the construct state it is considered as forming with the verb a kind of compound; and when in the casal form, it is either a noun of manner, an adverbial expression, or a noun in apposition.

Neuter verbs take sometimes the indirect object as direct object without preposition.

The third person plural is used as indeterminate as in English: *iḳbū*, "they say," "it is said."

The various moods are irregularly used, because the notion of their value seems to have been lost at an early date, as that of the case-endings in the noun; but the following principles may be given, though in practice they were often ignored.

The infinitive is not really a mood; its forms, infinitive simple and the four participles, are treated as nouns.

The permensive carries an idea of continuity; it expresses an action the effect of which is still lasting when the narration takes place; for this reason it has neither past, present, nor future.

The indicative is the narrative mood *par excellence.* It is the one by which any statement is made. The shortness of its forms give a great vivacity to the narration.

The subjective is more solemn, and might be called the oratory mood; it ought to be used for principal sentence only.

The dependent mood is used in secondary relative sentences, or in secondary sentences beginning by a conjunction like *ki*, *šumma*, &c.

The objective mood is used generally in secondary sentences brought on as a consequence of the principal; but is often confounded with the previous mood; from its consequential value it sometimes implies the idea of futurity.

The energetic mood is composed of archaic forms. It gives strength to the meaning of the verb, but does not alter it; it has forms corresponding to the three previous moods, *um* corresponding to *u*, *im* to *i*, and *am* to *a*, and ought to be used accordingly, but these energetic forms are rare in the modern texts, and their use not always consistent.

The paragogic is merely the previous mood with the addition of the enclitic *ma*, which generally implies a consequence, and ought to be followed by the objective mood; in many cases the enclitic, however, simply represents the copula, and the double *m* is the consequence of the accent being thrown back on the previous vowel.

The aorist expresses the past; it is used sometimes, but rarely, for the permensive with an idea of continuity.

The mutative is used for the present and future; and also in a very few cases, when the narration represents the action as actually taking place, for the past; but in that case it is only a figure of speech.

The imperative is used for command, but the precative expresses only a wish.

The infinitive simple can be used for the future: *la epišu*, "he will not do."

The Kal gives the primary meaning of the stem or theme.

The Niphal has generally the passive meanings of the Kal; in other cases a developed meaning.

ikkibuš (for *inkibus*), "he was conquered," from *kabāšu*, "to trample upon;" *iššaknu*, "they were made or placed," from *šakānu*, *naptāru*, "to defend," from *patāru*, "to free."

The Shaphel is mostly used as a factitive or causative: *ušeškin*, "he caused to be placed or he established, and he caused to be made or he achieved," from *šakānu*; *ušaklil*, "he caused to be completed, *i.e.*, he finished," from *kalālu*, "to be complete."

The Pael gives to the stem an intensitive meaning, or simply emphasises the primary meaning, and is rarely used as a causative. On account of its intensitive character it has often the same meaning as the Kal, and its tenses are used for those of the Kal, especially with the weak verbs: *ušakkan*, "I placed," from *šakānu*; *luḫallik*, "may he destroy," from *ḫalāku*, "to injure;" *uparrir*, "I dispersed," from *parāru*, "to hinder;" *uḳubbu*, "he says," from *ḳabū*.

The secondary voices have often a reflective force, and indicate that the action is done by the subject for himself; it may also be used as passive. Sometimes their force is simply intensitive: *iktanak*, "he places his own seal," "he seals for himself," from *šakānu*, "to seal;" *iḳtabi*, "he declared or spoke for himself," from *ḳabū*, "to speak;" *ultaḳṣiru*, "they assembled," lit. "they caused to come together for themselves," from the Shaphel of *ḳaṣāru*, "to collect;" *uptehir*, "he gathered," from *paḫaru*, "to collect;" *iptalḫu*, "they shall fear," from *palāḫu*, "to fear;" *iḫtalik*, "he was injured," from *ḫalāku*, "to injure."

The tertiary voices have a frequentative meaning or express energy: *iḫtanabbatu*, "they go about plundering," from *ḫabātu*; *ittanallaka*, "he goes repeatedly," N³ from *alāku*, "to go."

The negative *la* is put before nouns, adjectives, and verbs. In composition it corresponds to the English "un:" *la-magiri*, "un-obedient;" and forms negative nouns, *la mami*, the "no-waters," that is "the want of water."

The negative *ul* is placed exclusively before verbs, and the negative *aa* forms prohibitives with the verbal forms.

Lu prefixed to the verb gives it a past meaning. This mode of expressing the past is only used in a few inscriptions of the time of Hammurabi and of the second Ninevite Empire.

The postfix *-ni* is placed after the verb (and after the pronominal suffix when there is one) to give to the sentence a dependent character. It is even to be found at the end of a sentence beginning with *ki*, "if."

The copula *u* is used to join two nouns or two sentences when they are treated as being in apposition.

The enclitic *ma* is only placed after the verb, and implies a consequence; sometimes, however, it has only the force of the simple copula.

The conjunction *lū* is distributive: *lu* . . *lu* . . *lu* . . "either . . . or . . . or." It has also the force of "whether" repeated.

SYNTAX OF SENTENCES.

The disposition of the words in the sentence is freer that in Akkadian; the formula would therefore vary. In the simple period, or in the principal sentence of a complex period, the same order as in Akkadian is often observed, that is, the formula dt-dp-ds-r-s-o-i-c-v. This order is generally followed in the bilingual texts, the object of the scribe having apparently been to give in most cases the nearest translation possible.

The direct object is often placed before the subject. This happens especially in private contracts, and when greater importance is given to the object.

The qualificative, either an adjective, a noun in apposition, or a noun with a preposition, follows the word it qualifies. The exceptions to this rule are exceedingly rare.

The indirect object very seldom precedes the subject, and follows sometimes the direct object. It is placed generally before the verb, but also may follow it.

The complement explaining the action of the verb is always placed near it.

When the direct object or the indirect object is represented by a pronominal suffix, it naturally always follows the verb. When it is a flexional pronoun (*iâši*, *iâti*, &c.), it often also follows the verb.

The reason of the action is generally placed before the subject and the objects, rarely between the subject and the objects, but often also after the verb.

The determinative of time, place, and state is placed at the beginning of the sentence.

In a secondary sentence, especially when introduced by the enclitic *ma* suffixed to the verb of the principal sentence, the order of the words is reversed: the verb stands first and is followed by the objects; sometimes even the subject is placed after the verb; the most common order is v-s-o-i.

Complex Period.

It has been observed that the moods correspond to the different forms of the nouns; these nominal forms were no doubt the origin of the characteristics of the moods, and analogy guided the writer in the use of them; but as the casal endings of the noun were so weakened as to acquire the obscure sound of a mute *ĕ* and were then confounded, so were the characteristics of the moods. The moods having become in this way undistinguishable to the ear, it threw great confusion in their use, and that is the reason why the forms of the subjective are found when we ought to expect the dependent or the objective, those of the indicative irregularly employed for the others, &c.

Regularly the indicative answers to the construct state and ought to be used only when the principal sentence in which it is employed requires a secondary consequential sentence, having its verb in the dependent mood.

The subjective was at first reserved for the principal sentence when it was complete in itself and did not necessarily require other complementary sentences. In the usage, however, it acquired a mere idea of importance, and secondary sentences were put in this mood to give them preëminence in the narration.

When a secondary sentence is introduced by a conjunction, it ought regularly to have its verb in the dependent mood; it is also the mood to use in a secondary sentence in apposition, if this sentence is considered as the immediate consequence of the principal sentence. A dependent sentence (that is, one having the verb in the dependent mood) precedes the principal.

The objective sentence generally follows the principal; it may be put in simple apposition or connected by the enclitic *ma* added to the verb of the preceding principal.

When an objective sentence is introduced by a flexional pronoun in the accusative, but used as subject (*iāti*, *kāti*, &c.), it precedes the principal or governing sentence.

When the principal sentence follows a secondary sentence introduced by a conjunction, its verb is often put in the objective mood, because the action is considered as the natural sequence of the statement made in the conjunctive sentence.

The conjunctive sentences often represent the determinatives of time, place or state, and must therefore precede the principal.

When two sentences are placed in apposition, the verb of the first one is often put in the indicative (mood of the construct), being to a certain extent considered as the complement explaining the second, just as the complement explaining the action of the verb is put in the construct state. In that case the second sentence ought to have its verb in the dependent mood.

When a sentence is followed by the enclitic *-ni* suffixed to its verb, it indicates generally a statement, the consequence of which is expressed by the principal sentence.

(1) *Šumā ablu-šu ša Šumu-iddina abil Gaḫal*, (2) *ultu Elamti kī iḫliḳu*, (3) *adi Taḫḫa' ittalka*, (4) *Taḫḫa' ḳata-šu kī aṣbata*, (4) *ultebiraššu*; (6) *maruṣ*; (7) *adi zime-šu mala iṣabbatu*, (8) *ana šarri enīa ašapparaššu.*

"(As to) Suma son of Sumuiddina son of Gahal, he had fled then from Elam, he went to the Tahha, I took him (*lit.* his hands) from the Tahha, I brought him back; he is ill, when he will have resumed his complete health, I will send him to the king, my lord."

This example taken from a letter-tablet is very important. There are two periods: in the first one extending to (6) all the verbs are in the aorist, the first sentence (1) having no verb plays the part of a determinative, the second is the principal, and its verb is in the subjective mood, the three others (3, 4 and 5) are considered as sequence, and their verbs are therefore in the objective mood. The second period begins by a permensive (6) playing the part of a determinative, in the two other sentences the verbs are in the future, the first (7) is the principal and therefore in the subjective mood, and the second, (8) the sequence, in the objective mood.

(1) *Uāteʿ maruštu imḫar-šu-ma ediššu innabit ana Nabāti* (2) *Uāteʿ ablu Hazailu aḫi abi ša Uāteʿ ablu Pir-Rammanu raman-šu iškunu ana šarruti Arabi;* (3) *Aššur ṭemu ušanni-ma* (4) *illika adi maḫrīa.*

"Misfortune happened to him, Uate, and he fled to Nabata, Uāte, son of Hazailu brother of the father of Uate son of Pirrammanu, made himself king of Arabia, Assur gave an order so that he came to my presence."

The first part of the period is the determinative of time and state and is in the indicative, or construct mood, the second is the statement and is in the subjective mood, the third is the consequence and is in the dependent mood, and the fourth, the final result, is in the objective mood.

Ilani rabuti iāti Aššurbanapla palaḫ-šun ana sapaḫ Elamti umaʿiru. "The great gods deputed me their worshipper to destroy Elam."

The following are two examples of very quick narrations; the subject is often thrown after the verb, and the verbs are most of them in the indicative or construct mood:

(1) *Innindu-ma šarrani kilallan ippušu taḫaza* (2) *ina biri-šunu innapiḫ išatu,* (3) *ina turbuʿti-šunu naʾduru pan Šamši,* (4) *ašamšatu iṣṣanunda* (5) *isar meḫu* (6) *ina miḫie taḫazi-šunu itla bel narkabti ippallasa šanā ša itti-šu.* (1) "The kings of the

two regions gathered so that they made battle, (2) among them fire blazed, (3) the face of the sun was darkened (subj. mood) with their clouds of dust, (4) a hurricane had gathered (objective mood, may be translated: having gathered), (5) the storm broke (construct mood, answers to the determinative of state), (6) in the storm of their battle the warrior charioteer does not recognise (subj. mood) his companion (lit. the other who is with him).

(1) *Ina pī Ištar u Rammani, ilani bēlī taḫazi limutte,* (2) *lu ana šarri Elamti* (3) *iteziz mati-šu,* (4) *ū šarru Nabuku-durrizur ittašiz* (5) *ina liti iṣabat Elamti ištalal šagaša.* (1) "By the command of Istar and Rimmon, the gods lords of battle evil rose (2) be it with the King of Elam! (3) his country was taken (4) and Nabuchadnezzar joined (him) (5) with might he took Elam (and) confiscated his goods."

(1) *Iati Sin-aḫe-irib šar Aššuri epiš šipri šuatu* (2) *ki ṭem ilani ina uznīa ipši-*(3)*ma kabatti ublam-*(4)*ma tenišit Kaldi ša ana nirīa la kitnušu assuḫam-*(5)*ma umšikki ušašši-šunuti-*(6)*ma ilbinu libitti* (7) *apikupe ša kirib Kaldi akšid-*(8)*ma appari-šun šamḫuti ina baḫulati nakiri kišitti ḳatīa ušaldida ana epiš šipri-ša.*

(2) "When the command of the gods came to my ears (3) so that it was important (1) that myself, Sennacherib, king of Assyria, should do this work, (4) therefore I removed the people of Chaldea who (were) unsubmissive to my yoke, (5) so I cause them to carry burdens (6) so that they should make bricks; (7) I took baskets from the middle of Chaldea (8) so I caused the best wicker to be brought by the rebel people captured by my hands to do its work."

In this example each sentence is introduced by *ma* as being a consequence of the preceding one. In sentence (7) the verb is in the indicative or construct mood, because it is a kind of determinative, "I took or having taken," and the verb of the next sentence is in the objective mood as being the result of the preceding one.

The following are two examples from a private contract, a statement before court:

Binaddunatan ana aššutu iršan-ni-ma šalšu mana kašpi nudunnā ilkie-ma edit martu ulid-šu. "Binaddunatan had me to wifehood, so he took three mana of silver, my dowry, and so I bore him one daughter."

ịatu u mutīa nadanu ū maḥari ina eli nudunniea nepuš-ma šamna ḳane bitu ebšu irṣitim aḥulā gallā kirib Barsip ana tišit šūššanu mana kašpi, adi šane mašu mana kašpi ša ultu Iddin-Marduk ana nišḥu niššam-ma ina šim biti šuatu niddidin-ma itti aḥameš nimḥur ina šatti arbati Nabunaʿid šar Babili.

"Myself and my husband we made selling and buying with the money of my dowry, namely: eight canes (ground and) a ruined house, territory of a large estate within Borsippa, for nine and two-thirds mana of silver, we made up the amount with two (and) a half mana of silver, which (was borrowed) from Iddinmarduk, (added) to the former, so we gave (it) as price of that house, in this way we traded together in the fourth year of Nabonidus, king of Babylon."

The last sentence from *itti aḥameš* really governs all the preceding ones; it might be translated, "we traded in this way: that I and my husband," &c.

VANNIC GRAMMAR.

PHONETIC.

THE Vannic alphabet is the same as in Akkadian and Assyrian; this is naturally the result of its syllabary being borrowed from Nineveh, and may only be but apparent, as the value of the characters have been found by comparing the signs given in the inscriptions with those of the Assyrian syllabary.

In deciphering many things are to be taken into account.

A great use is made of determinative perfixes, or, as better termed, of ideograms followed either by the phonetic complement or by the phonetic determinative (*i.e.*, the whole word written phonetically). In some cases, however, the ideograms are used, as in Akkadian and Assyrian, without any complement or determinative. There was a tendency to the alphabetism, so that the vowel is often repeated after a syllabic sign ending in a vowel, even when it is not long; and the final vowel of a syllable is not to be read in some cases, being given merely, because the characters being syllabic, the consonant could not be written alone. All the inscriptions do not belong to the same region, and some show dialectical variations. One inscription gives *bi* for *ni*, in another the guttural *ḥ* is dropped: *aldiš* for *ḥaldiš*. The documents are still too scanty to enable us to give the rules of such changes.

The vowels are often assimilated. As in Assyrian, when two vowels are not assimilated it may be due to the presence of an aspirate, which is not written. The two letters *ī* and *ē* are confounded. The consonants *b* and *p* are often confounded, so are also *ṣ* and *z*, *d* and *ṭ*. A dental between two vowels is easily dropped.

The vowels are lengthened generally by the addition of the letter *e*, *ae* = *ā*, *ie* = *ī*, &c., but often *aa*, *ai* are found for *ae* (*ā*), *ii* for *ie* (*ī*), &c. The vowel *u* seems to have had sometimes the value of the semi-vowel *v* (or *w*): *ua*, *ue*, *ui*, *uu*, might represent *va*, *ve*, *vi*, *vu*.

FORMS OF THE WORDS.

Nouns and Adjectives.

In Vannic there are two genders and two numbers, but neither gender nor number are distinguished clearly, from the grammatical point of view.

All nouns are appellatives, and may be either substantives or adjectives. The relations of the nouns to the other words and the special extension of the meaning attached to them are indicated by means of suffixes.

The nominal stems are always terminated by a vowel, *a*, *i*, or *u*, but are never found without suffix. The simplest form is that of the noun in the dependent case answering, in a certain measure, to the construct state of the Semitic tongue. This case is formed by lengthening the final vowel of the stem: *esi*, "law," dependent case, *esī*, *giššūri*, "mighty," d.c., *guššūrie*.

The suffixes may be followed by the enclitic demonstrative pronoun *ni*. The most important are the following:

(1.) *š*, which is added to the vowel of the noun; its full form is *ši*, and formed primitively names of state, but was to a great extent used to denote the nominative: *Ḥaldi-š*, *Menua-š*.

(2.) *di*, forms names of agents, and is used also to form a kind of locative: *kuṭa-di*, "on leaving."

(3.) *li* (formerly read *da*), forms local names: from *pi*, "name," *pi-li*, "a memorial," *lit.* "the place of the name."

(4.) *ki*, forms instrumentals, and for this reason is often to be translated by an adverb: *ali-ki*, "partly;" *kau-ki*, "with weapons." In some cases it is written *kid*, perhaps for *ki-di*, the second suffix being superposed.

(5.) *li*, indicates that the action is made after the completion of the object taking this suffix, and has been called the perfective case: *meš̌u-li*, "after the libations;" *zatua-li*, "after the gate (was built)."

(6.) *ḥi*, forms patronymics, and also names of people, belonging to or followers of: *Išpūni-ḥi-ni*, "the son of Ispunis;" *Eria-ḥi*, "son of Erias;" *tu-ḥi*, "captive."

(7.) *na*, indicates the country: *Ḥaldiš-na*, "of the land of Haldis;" *Ḥati-na*, "of the land of the Hati."

(8.) *a*, forms names of population or collectives: *Ḥaldi-a*, "the Haldians;" *ḥaradi-a*, "armies."

(9.) *ka*, forms gentilic names, but having a more limited extension, and forms also serial names: *Agišti-ka*, "the family of Agistis."

(10.) *ue* (to be read perhaps *ve*), marks the possession: *ḥula-ue*, "having kings."

(11.) *ṣi*, marks relation: *asi-ṣi*, "that which belongs to the cavalry."

There are few other suffixes, very rare in the inscriptions: *zi*, in *armu-zi*, "altar," perhaps another form of *š* or *ṣi*; *ri*, an individualising suffix, more used in the cognate tongues; *bi*, found in *ati-bi*, "thousands," and *niri-bi*, "dead," &c.

The suffixes can be superposed, that is, a derived word formed by means of a suffix may take the suffixes as a primitive word, so we have for instance: *ḥuradi*, "soldier" (this word being no doubt itself a derivation of *ḥura*); *ḥura-di-a*, "soldiery;" *ḥura-di-ni-li*, "camp;" *ḥura-di-ni-li-ue*, "belonging to the camp," &c.

NUMERALS.

The numerals are always written ideographically. The only one found written phonetically is *atibi*, "thousands *or* myriads."

It is only to be noticed that the word for "thousand" seems to have been repeated after each number. For instance, 23,000 was written XXMIIIM, which implies that it was literally "twenty thousands (and) three thousands."

Of the ordinals we know *šušini*, "first," *tarani*, "second," and *šištini*, "third," evidently formed with the enclitic *ni*.

DEMONSTRATIVES.

The demonstrative mostly used is *i*, followed by the enclitic *ni*: *ini*, "this;" *e͑a* may only be another form of the same.

išti, "this" and *uli*, "that," are not so much used. Both can take the enclitic *ni* and all the suffixes, like the nouns, and be used as abstracts: *išti-ni-ue-di-a*, "the people belonging to them." Properly *uli* means "another."

šuḥe, "these," which appears to be invariable, seems to be formed from *ša*, the correlative of *ini*; *ša* receives itself the suffixes and the enclitic: *ša-ue*, "belonging there."

The distributive is *manu*: *aṣuš manuš*, "every mouth;" *ali manu*, "some and each." With the enclitic *u* is assimilated *mani-ni*.

For "some . . . some," *ali-ki* . . . *ali-ki*, primitively "partly . . . partly," is used.

PERSONAL PRONOUNS.

Of the personal pronouns only the first and third persons have been found; they may take the suffixes as a noun.

Nominative *me-š*, "the his" or "he" (himself).

Genitive or dependent *me-i*, "of him."

With the local suffix, *me-li* or *mei-ali*, "the place of it."

All the forms with suffixes may also take the enclitic *ni*: *mei-ši-ni*, "his, its," "what is his or its."

The possessive is found under the three forms, *mu*, *ma*, and *me*; the first is the one mostly used.

Of the first person only the nominative is found: *ieš*, "I."

VERB.

The Vannic verb has only one tense, the aorist, and only the first and third persons of it are known. The same form stands for the singular and plural of the third person, and the genders are not distinguished.

The infinitive, or *nomen verbi*, always ends in *u*:

kugu, "to write," or "the action of writing."

From it is formed the aorist with the suffix *bi* for the first person, and *ni* for the third sing. or plural:

kugu-bi, "I wrote."
kugu-ni, "he, she," or "they wrote."

A kind of gerund is formed by the suffix *li* or *lie*, which takes sometimes *a* as vowel of union, and is used for present or future:

du, "to destroy;" *du-li* or *du-lie*, "he destroys."

This form was no doubt used for all persons.

The present of the participle is formed from the infinitive by the suffix *eš* in the nominative:

šiu, "to remove," pres. part. *šī-eš* (for *šiu-eš*), "removing."

The past participle is formed by the suffix *aš* in the nominative:

zaduaš, "being built."

This, as the infinitive and the present participle, can take the suffixes:

zadua-li, "after being built."

A few examples are found of a form composed with the suffix *me;* these are imperatives or precatives:

asḫu-me, "may they occupy;"

A derivative causative voice is formed with the suffix *šu* or *ša*, which is then treated as an ordinary verb:

ḫa-šu-bi, "I cause to possess."
ḫurḫar-ša-bi, "I cause to be excavated."

The form *aptini*, "it is called," or "they call it," by the side of *tini*, "he called," has suggested the belief in a passive voice which would be formed by a prefix *ap;* but a formation by prefix is too much opposed to the genius of the language, it is preferable to see another stem, perhaps a compound one, in *aptini.*

ADVERBS.

As in Akkadian the adverbs are formed by means of the postpositions or suffixes added to nouns, demonstratives or pronouns, in fact many of the words having the suffixes may be considered as adverbs and translated by our adverbs of time, place or state:

ali-ki, "partly;" *ši-li*, "after dawn;" *kuta-di*, "at the departure;" *ini-li*, "here;" *manu-li*, "in each place;" *ušta-di*, "in approaching;" *'ā-li*, "for sacrifice."

As in Assyro-Babylonian nouns and pronouns in the dependent and nominative cases, and even with the enclitic pronoun *ni*, are used as adverbs:

> *gunušā*, "as a spoil;" *ainei*, "with dust;" *iu*, "thus;" *aie*, "in the land;" *šidi-š*, "anew;" *ardi-ni*, "during the day = publicly;" *nara-ni*, "with fire."

pari or *parie* requires a special mention; primitively an adjective, it has come to mean "out of," and to be used apparently as a preposition.

The negative has not been found yet.

CONJUNCTIONS.

There are two words to express the copula, *ui* and *ali*.

SYNTAX.

As already stated, the gender was not distinguished by any particular forms in the nouns or adjectives; in the cases of proper names, as in Assyrian, those of men were preceded by the straight wedge, and those of women by the sign of female. The plural was not distinguished either, but merely indicated by the ideographic sign of "many" (which was probably not pronounced) placed after the word.

The demonstrative enclitic *ni* could be added to any nominal form, and has in a certain degree the same force as our article "the:" *ina-š*, "a city" (with *š*, the mark of the nominative), *inai-ni*, "the city."

Sometimes this enclitic seems to be used to indicate the accusative.

When a noun is used in the plural, an attempt has been made

in some cases to distinguish it from the singular by repeating the enclitic twice, as in Akkadian with the demonstrative *ne; gušu-ni-ni*, "the slaves."

When a noun is used in the dependent case, it is considered as forming a kind of compound word with the word from which it depends and precedes it: *Menuai pili*, "the memorial of Menuas."

The suffix *š*, when it marks the nominative, is only added to the word in the singular. For the plural the word is placed in the dependent case, or takes the enclitic simple or repeated.

The words used as adjectives are either considered as forming, with the noun they qualify, a kind of compound, or as being in apposition. In the first case they are placed in the dependent case and precede the qualified noun: *giššurie kuruni*, "the mighty giver." In the other case they follow the qualified noun, and take the same suffix: *aṣuš manu-š*, "each mouth;" *Ḫaldie eurie*, "Haldis, the lord."

R. The word with a suffix is considered often as a derivative word, and being then treated as a new stem, can take the *š* of the nominative and the other suffixes: *Išpūini-š Saridurie-ḫi-ni-š*, "Ispunis Sariduris's son;" *Ḫaldini-ni alsuiši-ni*, "the numerous Haldians."

Sometimes the word used adjectively is considered as giving an explication in parenthesis, so to say; then it takes the enclitic *ni*, and may or may not have the same suffixes as the noun explained by it: *Menua-š, Išpuni-ḫi-ni*, "Menuas, the Ispunian (son of Ispunis)." *Ḫaldi-a išti-ni*, "the people of Haldi, these."

The regimen of an adjective generally follows it: *Karuni ebanie*, "who has given the countries."

The same rule applies to participles and all words used adjectively.

When the participle has a suffix, its regimen takes the same suffix: *šia-di Eriaḫinie ebanie-di*, "in despoiling the Erianians' land;" *ušta-di Urme-di*, "in approaching Urme."

The numerals stand before the nouns: III *ašida*, "3 palaces;" LX *tumeni*, "60 villages."

The demonstratives are considered as adjectives, and follow the same rules, but they may be used abstractly.

The personal pronoun is really an abstract noun, and follows the same rules.

The possessive pronoun follows the noun possessed: *ikukani mu*, "his goods."

The relative pronoun is always understood; the incidental sentence is placed in apposition (see SYNTAX OF SENTENCES).

The verb distinguishes neither genders nor numbers: *ti-ni*, "he, she, or they called."

The gerund used as present, future, and conditional is invariable. It is also used as precative.

The infinitives and participles are treated as nouns and adjectives.

The word *pari*, which has the meaning of a kind of preposition, must be considered as an adjective governing a noun, and its use becomes quite regular according to the Vannic grammar.

SYNTAX OF SENTENCES.

The Vannic language has been strongly influenced by Assyrian, and the order of the words in the sentence is nearly the same as in the latter.

The verb is placed at the end of the sentence, the object follows the subject, the name of manner, that is the complement, precedes immediately the verb; the reason of the action is placed either at the head of the sentence before the subject, especially if it is a proper name, or follows the verb (as in Assyrian) if it is a name of action. The determinatives of time, place, and state are placed at the head of the sentence. The indirect object is confounded with the reason of the action; when both are expressed in the same sentence, the reason of the action is considered to be a qualificative of the indirect regimen.

Kudaia-di parie Bīa Ḫušani ušta-bi, "on departing from the land of Bias, I conquered the land of Husas."

Ḫaldie ḫali XVII *paḫini*, "to (or for) Haldis for sacrifice seventeen oxen (I gave)."

Ḫaldie eurie ini pulūsie Menuaš kuguni, "to Hadis the lord Menuas wrote this inscription."

Complex sentences are rare. As a rule the sentences follow one another without being connected in any grammatical way. Two sentences may be connected by the copula *ui*, more rarely with the copula *ali*. When sentences follow one another without copula, they may be considered as being in apposition. When several sentences follow one another, especially in the case of an enumeration, the verb given in the first one is not repeated in the others.

When an incidental sentence marks the time or state, represents in fact the determinative, it is rendered by the infinitive with the suffix *li* (compare Akkadian). When two sentences are placed in apposition, the order of the members of the second are often reversed as in Assyrian. After the verb "to say" or "to speak" the incidental sentence is sometimes introduced by the adverb *iu*, "thus," following the verb, but more often this adverb is understood.

Ḫaldinini Menuaš armani atḫuli šidištuali, Ḫaldinini alsunini Menuaš ali : aluš ini armanili tulie, aluš pitulie, aluš ainiei inili dulie, aluš uliš tiulie, ieš zadub turinini, Ḫaldiš mani, pini mei, arḫiurulini mei, inani mei nara aue ululie. "Menuas has restored the destroyed tablets for the Haldians, to the numerous Haldians Menuas says : 'whoever will carry away these tablets, whoever will deface (them), whoever will thrust (them) in the dust, whoever will undo that I did on the rock, may Haldis consign to fire (and) water, (*i.e.*, burn and drown or obliterate), himself, his name, his family, (and) his town.'"

Ḫaldinini Menuaš alie iu : Manaidi ebania tubi, amaštubi ikukani ḫuradinili. "Menuas spoke to the Haldians thus : 'in approaching the land of the Minni, I carried away the population, I plundered the goods, the camp.'"

Ebania tubi, inanie abilidubi, IIIMCCLXX *taršuanie aliki zašgubi, aliki šeḥira agubi,* CLXX *nauuše parubi,* LXII *diṭuni,* IIMCCCCXI *paḥini,* VIMCLX *šuše.* "I carried off the population, I burned the cities, of 3270 soldiers I slew some, I took some alive, I carried off 170 horses, 62 camels, 2411 oxen, 6140 sheep."

Nu aliisi ikukaniedini šaue, nanuli mei ašei piurtani, ḥaidiani teriḥinie saridurini tini, saridurini uduliei aue, Seḥaulie ūni urulie kurienini uiduš suni. "(When) the king (had been) assembling the wealthy people of there, he chose the site for his temple, he named the workmen working for Sariduris, Uidus gratuitously provided those (working) for Sariduris at the monument with water from Sahauli (*i.e.*, the place of Sehaus), and with food from (his) household."

These few sentences will serve as illustrations of simple and complex periods. The last one is especially interesting, because it is not imitated from those found on the Assyrian monuments. From it it appears that the king Sariduris, wishing to have a temple built, imposed taxes on the wealthy people, and task on the poorer class of the neighbourhood, and that a certain man, Uidus, provided to the working men water, brought from a place called Sehauli, and food from his own household; for this reason the king thought that he deserved to have his name recorded.

It is to be noticed that in the last sentence of the period, which may be considered as the principal, the subject, *Uiduš*, is placed immediately before the verb; perhaps we have here the primitive order of the sentence in Vannic before it was influenced by Assyrian. The expression *kurienini suni* "provided gratuitously" might be translated "gave as a gift;" what is meant is that Uidus did not charge anything.

MEDIC GRAMMAR.

PHONETIC.

THE Medic alphabet is the same as in Akkadian, except for the three consonants *ḳ*, *ṣ*, and *ṭ*, which are not represented.

Among the vowels *aa* represents *ā*; *e* and *i* are easily confounded; the letter *u* was perhaps pronounced sometimes as *ü*. There are two signs for this vowel *u* isolated, and it is supposed that one of them represented *o*, but this is doubtful.

The consonants offer the same confusion as in Akkadian at the end of a closed syllable, the same sign representing *ab* and *ap*, &c. The consonants seem also to have often been confounded at the beginning. It is supposed with some reason that all the letters of the same order were confounded. As certain sounds cannot be expressed, it has been supposed that in certain cases the vowel was not to be pronounced; for instance, *gi-ud* standing for *gid*, *ku-ir* for *kur*, &c. This must have been the case in some instances, but according to the rule we have taken, we give the spelling given by the inscriptions, and write *kuir*, although it may have been pronounced *kur* or *kir*.[1]

FORMS OF THE WORDS.

NOUNS AND ADJECTIVES.

There are two genders and two numbers; the genders are not distinguished by any special forms, and the plural is often the same as the singular.

[1] Many words are preceded by a straight wedge or a determinative prefix aphone; this is indicated in our transcription by a capital letter.

F

All stems, nominal and verbal, end in a vowel. The words are built from these stems by means of suffixes, and their relations are also indicated in the same way.

The bare stem is used to form certain compounds with other words, and for this reason represents the dependent case of Vannic or the construct of the Semitic tongues. The suffixes are added to this dependent case, and the stems with a suffix constitute a new word which can take other suffixes.

The suffixes are :—

(1.) *r*, *ri*, or *ra* (primitively a demonstrative) forms nouns and adjectives, or is simply added to the noun to individualise its meaning: *irša*, "great;" *irša-ra*, "chief."

(2.) *n*, *ni*, or *na* (primitively a demonstrative, cf. Vannic enclitic *ni*) forms principally adjectives of manner, but also substantives: *niman*, "belonging to;" *Kurašna*, "of Cyrus, Cyrusian."

(3.) *k*, *ki*, or *ka* forms adjectives and substantives, especially abstracts: *mišni-ka*, "bad;" *tidu-k*, "falsehood;" *ḫari-ki*, "scarce."

R. The consonant of these three suffixes may be doubled, and we have *iršarra*, *ḫarikki*, &c.

(4.) *da* forms adjectives and substantives, but also is used as definite article: *marri-da*, "all;" *mar-da*, "the right;" *adda-da*, "the father."

(5.) *ti* or *tu*, perhaps the same as the preceding, used especially to form name of country: *zi-tu*, "so," from *zi*, "to see;" *Apir-ti* (part of Susiana), "Apirtia."

(6.) *maš* (perhaps compound of *ma* and *š*) forms abstracts: *Ain-maš*, "royalty;" *duki-ummaš* (from *du*, "to be"), "cause."

(7.) *ma* (primitively "place" or "country") forms the locative of the nouns.

(8.) *š* (abbreviated form of *maš*, or more probably primitive suffix forming this one with the precedent) forms a few adverbs: *ukda-š*, "above," really "the above."

Some words appear also to be formed by prefixes; a very characteristic one is *ḫa*, which implies futurity: *ḫa-ḫudda*, "to become," from *ḫudda*, "to do."

As stated above, the suffixes can be superposed; so from *ma* and *r* we get *mar*, used to express a kind of ablative. The combination of *ka*, *ma*, and *r* gives *kamar*, meaning "far from."

A certain number of words (nouns, adjectives, and adverbs) are used after nouns in the dependent case, and have been considered as postpositions, but these words are really used as abstracts, and form, with the preceding word, compounds: *Barsir-kir*, lit. "Persian-one," *i.e.*, "a Persian."

The use of *idaka*, really a substantive meaning the action of standing, but employed as postposition to express "with," is to be explained in the same way, as also the locative postfix *ma*.

The plural is formed by the suffix *pi* or *bi*, added to the bare form of the singular; sometimes the final vowel is dropped, in other cases the *p* or *b* is doubled. The suffixes are added to the plural as to the singular.

When a new stem is formed by means of a suffix the characteristic of the plural is added after it.

With the ideograms the plural is indicated by the sign of the plural read perhaps *meš*.

NUMERALS.

The numerals are always written by means of ciphers, their pronunciation is therefore unknown.

We only find in the texts *kir* used as a postfix to express the indefinite article "a," which may be also the number "one." The expression *šamakmar*, "twice," is also found; the number "two" may have been *šama* or *šamak*.

The ordinals are formed by adding *ummaš* to the cardinals: v-*ummas*, "5th."

DEMONSTRATIVES.

The demonstrative mostly used with the noun is *ḥi;* this form is really the objective case, but the nominative *ḥu* is found only in composition to form demonstrative pronouns: *ḥu-pirri*, "this one," plural *ḥupibi*, "these ones."

From the same stem is derived *ḥubi*, "that," used only for things (as the French *cela*), and always in the objective case. Other forms are obtained from these derivatives. From *ḥupibi*, "these," we have with the suffix *na* an adjectival form *ḥupibi-na*, "the theirs" or "theirs;" from *ḥubi* we have *ḥubi-da*, "that thing."

Another demonstrative pronoun is *akka*, "this," used also as interrogative and relative pronoun. The plural is *akkabi*.

The relative pronoun is *appa*, invariable.

PERSONAL PRONOUNS.

The personal pronouns are:

1st pers. sing.	*U*[1]	plur. *Nuku*.
2nd pers. sing.	*Nu*	plur. *manka*.
3rd pers. sing.	*ḥupirri*	plur. *Appi*.

The pronouns of the first and second persons in the singular were used as nominatives or objectives, but to mark the objective case an *n* might be added; *U* becomes then *ūn* (written *U-un*), and *Nu Nuin*.

The pronoun of the third person was no doubt originally *irri* or *iri* but took for support a demonstrative and became *ḥupi-irri*, but the original form is preserved in the objective case, which is *ir*.

The objective case of the first and second persons of the plural is not known, but in the third person it is regularly formed, *appin* or *apin*, "them."

[1] Found once written *Ḥu*.

These pronominal stems can take the suffixes like the nominal stems; so we have *U-ni-na*, "the mine;" *appi-ni*, "the theirs;" *U-ikki*, "the I," *i.e.*, "myself," used as dative; *ap-ir* or *appi-ir*, "the they," used for "to them," *U-ikki-mar*; "from me," &c.

Suffixes derived from the pronouns serve to express the possessive: *mi* (*wi* perhaps for *ui*), "my;" *ni*, "thy;" and *ri*, "his."

The forms for the plural are not known.

For the first person *u* is also used as a possessive, but is prefixed to the noun: *karpi-mi* or *U-karpi*, "my hand."

There are other forms—really nominal or adjectival forms—which are used to express possession or connection, as *Nukami* "the ours." Of the same class is *nudami* (also written once *daminu*), which refers to the third person, though it would rather appear to be a derivative of the second.

VERBS.

All the verbal stems end in one of the three vowels *a*, *i*, and *u*. This distinction forms three conjugations: 1st conj. *dana*, "to give," 2nd conj. *tiri*, "to say," 3rd conj. *iazu*, "to pray."

From each stem voices are formed by adding certain suffixes:

nunú for the desiderative.
manlu for the reciprocal.
na for the causative.
da for the emphatic.

New derivatives may be formed from these voices; so we have the desiderative of the causative formed by adding *nunú* to *na*: *nanunú*, &c.

Besides these voices the verbs are divided into active and neuter, taking different sets of suffixes to form the persons of the tenses. When the same stem takes the two forms, the neuter has the force of passive.

For the active and transitive verb there are two principal

tenses, which serve to form the others. The present forms the future and the imperative. The past forms the imperfect, pluperfect, and precative.

The personal suffixes of the present are :—

Singular.

1st pers.	2nd pers.	3rd pers.
-man,	*-mainti,*	*-manra* or *-manri.*

Plural.

1st pers.	2nd pers.	3rd pers.
-manūn,	*-maintip,*	*-mampi.*

The future is formed by dropping the syllable *ma*, so we have 1st pers. *n*, 2nd pers. *inti*, &c.

R. The *n* of the 1st person in these two tenses is sometimes replaced by the syllable *ra*: *mara* for *man*.

The imperative is formed by changing *man* of the 1st pers. of the present into *š* for the 2nd pers. sing. and plur., the only one used.

The personal suffixes of the past are :—

Singular.

1st pers.	2nd pers.	3rd pers.
a,	*ki,*	*š.*

Plural.

1st pers.	2nd pers.	3rd pers.
ūd,	[*kip ?*]	*aš* or *maš.*

R. The *a* characteristic of the first person is often absorbed by the ending vowel of the verbal stem, so that the first person is confounded in form with the latter. To prevent this confusion, the characteristic *a* is sometimes united to the stem by the semi-vowel corresponding to that of the stem, we have then with a stem in *a*, *'a* (the aspirate is not written *aa* for *a'a*); with a stem in *i*, *ia*; with a stem in *u*, *ma* (*wa*).

The neuter verbs have only one set of personal suffixes:

Singular.

1st pers.	2nd pers.	3rd pers.
giud,	*ikti*,	*ik*.

Plural.

1st pers.	2nd pers.	3rd pers.
giūd,	[*iktip*?]	*p*, or *ppi*.

The present takes these suffixes with the syllable *ma*; for the past they are joined to the stem directly. For verbs of this kind the present and future have the same form.

The other tenses are formed for the active and neuter verbs by suffixes added to the personal suffixes. These suffixes are:

ra for the imperfect.
da for the pluperfect.
ni for the precative.

The inscriptions do not of course give examples of all the forms with the same stem.

From *ḥudda*, "to do," we find *ḥudda*, "I did;" *ḥuddaš*, "he did;" *ḥuddaūd* and *ḥudtiūd*, "we did;" *ḥuddaš*, "they did;" *ḥuddara*, "I have done;" *ḥuddada*, "I had done;" *ḥuddašda*, "he had done;" *ḥuddūdda* "we had done;" *ḥuddak*, "he was done;" *ḥuddamara*, "I do;" *ḥuddiš*, "do;" *ḥuddimanra*, "he will do;" *ḥuddinunúba*, "they wished to do."

From *budda*, "to flee;" *buddaka*, "he fled;" *buddana*, "I caused to flee."

From *tida*, "to lie;" *tidinra*, "he will lie."

From *tiri*, "to say, to call," *tiri* and *tiria*, "I say;" *'tiriš*, "he says;" *tiriaš*, "they say;" *tirimanpi*, "they are called;" *tirimanūn*, "we are called;" *tirišti*, "they were called," &c.

There are few verbs which appear to have abnormal forms, but these are in some cases archaic, contracted or decayed. It must also be borne in mind that the flexions of the verb have grown out of the nominal and adjectival suffixes, and forms, which at one period were regularly employed with all the verbal stems, have maintained themselves with some verbs, when with others different suffixes have been preferred.

The verb *da*, "to do, to be, or to send,"[1] has preserved for the first person singular the archaic form *da'*, "I did;" but for the third we have *daiš* and *daš*, "he did." In the pluperfect the second person is a nominal formation with the pluperfect suffix *da-š-da*, lit. (thou) doer (wast).

The verb "to be" was primitively *gin*, but the *g* passed little by little into *y*, and disappeared, changing only the *i* into *e*. The *g* of this verb is the one preserved in the first persons of the neuter verbs *gi-ud*. We find it without the suffix in *na-n-gi*, "I say;" the other persons are regular: *na-inti*, "thou sayest;" *na-nri*, "he says."

The persons of the verb "to be" are very irregular, several suffixes being superposed to compensate the weakening. We have *ennugiud*, "I was;" *en-ri* and *en-ri-ir*, "he was;" *enbib*, *en-ri-p*, and *en-ri-pi*, "they were."

To *dašda* may be compared *bišda*, "he did;" the same root is perhaps to be found in *innuibbida*, "as long as thou wilt be able," which is difficult to explain.

dumane, "he was or he did," appears to be an adjectival formation from *da*.

ADVERBS.

The adverbs are formed from substantives, adjectives, and pronouns, with the suffixes *ikki* and *da*; but a great many other terminations are found, and nouns, adjectives, and pronouns may be used adverbially, without taking any particular ending.

From the demonstrative *ḥu* or *ḥi* are derived numerous adverbs: *ḥima*, "here;" *ḥami*, "there;" *ḥamimar*, "thence;"

[1] Thus three notions seem to have been connected in the minds of those who spoke this language.

ḥamašir, "then;" *ḥupamašir*, "now;" *ḥamak*, "how;" with *zitu*, "so;" *ḥizitu*, lit. "this so;" *ḥupaintuikkiummaš*, "consequently," &c.

šaššata, "previously;" *maššaka*, "latterly."

The negative is *inni*. The form *annu* or *anu* is used before verbs to express the prohibitive.

The word *badar*, which has been considered as a preposition, is no doubt an adverb or a noun: taken adverbially, it means "thoroughly" or "at last."

CONJUNCTIONS.

There are two words to express the copula "and," *āk* and *kudda*.

Other conjunctions are:

kuiš, "while;" *anka*, "if;" *sap*, "because," &c.

SYNTAX.

The Medic syntax offers many analogies with the Vannic. The genders are not distinguished by any special form.

The possessive or genitive is expressed in two ways. The governed noun, without flexion, is placed before the regent, forming with it a kind of compound word, and the regent takes the determinative suffix *ri*: *Kuraš šak-ri*, "the son of Cyrus;" or the regent stands first without flexion, and the governed noun takes the adjectival suffix *na*: *šak Kuraš-na*, lit. "son Cyrusian."

The adjective, or the noun used as such, follows the word qualified: it is really placed in apposition, and for this reason sometimes takes the same suffix as the noun it qualifies, but also may take others: *Nap iršarra*, "a great god;" *ukkurarra iršanna*, "the great universe."

When an adjective follows a plural it takes the plural suffix:

Ru'meš ḥarikkip, "a few men." But the plurals taken as abstracts are followed by the adjectives in the singular.

The words governed by an adjective or a participle precede it.

Two words, nouns or a noun and adjective, may be joined by the relative *appa*, "who, which:" *Daššutum appa Patipna*, "the rebel people," lit. "the people who (are) rebels."

The cardinal numerals precede the word in the plural: IX. *Ain-ip*, "nine kings;" XXIII. *Dāiauš*, "twenty-three provinces."

The ordinals follow the noun:

U IX-*ummaš*, "I the 9th."

To give the date the number—apparently the cardinal—precedes the word for "day," then comes the ideogram for "month," followed by the name of the month. As we have no document really national, but only those written by order of the Persian kings, these names of the months are the transcription of the Persian.

The demonstrative *ḥi* is invariable and placed after, rarely before, the noun; *ḥupirri* also follows or precedes the noun, but often has not the force of a demonstrative, and is used simply as an article.

The demonstratives derived from *ḥu* may be used abstractly without a noun and take the suffixes as the nouns.

The personal pronouns are considered as nouns and take the suffixes accordingly. That of the first person *U* may be used instead of *Un* as objective: *U daš*, "is to me." The objective case is used to express the direct or indirect object (accusative or dative).

Sometimes when the object of the verb is expressed a pronoun representing it is however placed before the verb, as in Akkadian. In this case the pronoun may be considered to be incorporated, and if the verb is a compound, the pronoun will be placed between the two elements of the word:

ema-ap-dušda, "he took them."

The tenses are not rigorously used, the present and future are often confounded.

Nouns and adjectives are with or without suffixes used

adverbially, that is, to express the complement of the verb or the determinative.

The negative is always placed before the verb, but the objective pronoun remains, when expressed, prefixed to the verb: the negative is therefore placed before it.

Of the two words meaning "and" *āk* is used especially at the beginning of a sentence and may be translated by "also;" the two words may be used together: *āk kudda*, "and also."

The conjunctions are placed at the beginning of the sentence.

Syntax of Sentences.

Long periods are avoided; they are, as a rule, cut into short sentences.

The order of the word in the sentence is *r-s-d-o-i-c-v*, but this order is not always observed. The reason of the action and the determinative of state are often confounded. The subject is often placed after the object, especially when the former is a pronoun. When the object is a personal pronoun it is always placed near the verb.

Uramašda ḥi Ain-maš U dunuiš, "Ormazd gave me this royalty."

mašni Pirrumartiš ḥupirri teulnuip ḥarikkip itaka buddukka, "then Phraortes, he having a few horsemen (*i.e.* with a few horsemen) fled."

Zaumin Uramašdana Daššutum appa Ḥunina Daššutum appa Bitipna iršeikki ḥalpiš, "by the favour of Ormazd the people who (were) mine killed in great (number) the people who (were) rebels."

mašni Nutiudbiul ḥupirri U Bapilu ḥalpīa, "then I killed this Nidintabel in Babylon."

Two sentences may be united by a copula *āk*, "and," or *kudda*. When the first sentence finishes with a verbal form ending in a consonant, this one takes the vowel *a* after being doubled to connect the second sentence. In that case (as with the enclitic *ma* in Assyrian) it implies that the action expressed by the verb of the second sentence is the consequence or result of the first.

Incidental sentences are introduced generally by the relatives *appa* or *akka;* sometimes the relative is understood, and the sentence is really placed in apposition explaining one word. In some cases words which might be introduced as an incidental sentence are treated as forming a long compound word; such a combination is often preceded by the demonstrative *ḥi.* The incidental relative or qualificative sentences are generally placed after the words they explain, being thus in the middle of the principal sentence.

The secondary sentences marking the time, the place or the state, are generally introduced by a conjunction ("when, as, if, while," &c.), and are placed before the principal.

āk šarak II-*ummaš-ma Bitip pirruir šairraib-ba šabarrakummaš Mimana idaka,* "and the second time the rebels gathered together (so that they fought) a battle with Mimana (lit. having Mimana)."

ḥupirri Daššutum Apir tituk-ka nanri, "this one lied to them, the people, (so that) he said."

Dāiauiš Markuiš ḥiše U-ikkimar biptibba Ru' kir Pirrada ḥiše Markuiš-irra ḥupirri Ain appini ir ḥuddaiš āk mašni U Daduršiš ḥiše Barsir kir U-Lubaruri Šakšaba manamaš Bakšiš ḥuddaš ḥuttik ḥupirrikki tingīa nangi, "the province, called Margiania, revolted (plur.) against me (so that) a man called Phrada, a Margian (rose and) this one they made king, and then I commissioned to the Persian, called Dadarses, my servant (who) had the satrapy of Bactriane, a messenger saying:"

āk anka Dippi ḥi innakkanuma ḥi zarinti inni kukirti Uramašda Nuin ḥalpišni āk kudda Numanmešni anu kitinti āk appa ḥuddainti apin Uramašda rippišni. "And if thou destroyest this inscription (and) these images (or figures), (if) thou dost not protect (them), may Ormazd kill thee, and also mayest thou have no offsprings, and may Ormazd curse (these things) which thou wilt do."

SUSIAN AND APIRIAN.

Susian (*i.e.* the language of the inscriptions of the old Elamite kings) and Apirian (*i.e.* that of the inscriptions of Mal-Amir) may be considered simply as dialects of Medic; and the latter being better known has been for convenience' sake taken as standard. The vocabulary and the grammar are to a great extent the same in the three dialects. Susian and Apirian have naturally in many cases more archaic forms; in others, however, they give examples of. a more advanced phonetical decay. It may also be concluded, from the use of parallel forms employed promiscuously in the very same texts, that Susian and Apirian never were systematised and fixed as literary languages; Medic, on the contrary, appears to have passed through such a process, probably at the court of the successors of Cyaxares, and no doubt under the influence of the mother tongue of the Aryan conquerors.

The phonetic changes between the three dialects are almost nil. Sometimes Apirian preserves the harder sounds, as in *dinku* = Medic, *dingi*, "to restore;" and sometimes has weaker forms, as *gani* = M. *kani*; *išni* = M. *mašni*, "then;" *uma* = M. *ḥuma*, "to create." Apirian has often the two forms hard and weakened: *ḥir* and *ir* = M. *ir*, "him." The changes of *b* and *p*, *t* and *d*, are difficult to register on account of the uncertainty of these sounds in Medic. Susian offers the same changes and variations as Apirian.

The nominal and adjectival formation is the same in the three dialects, and the suffixes are the same. The pronouns are also the same, as far as they are known; in Apirian the stronger form of the first person pronoun *ḥu* has been reserved to express the nominative "I" and *u* the accusative "me." The aspirate has been lost in Susian as in Medic.

For the verbal forms Susian and Apirian give also the same paradigm as Medic. But both dialects preserve in the greatest number of verbs the primitive aspirate to mark the first person of the first singular in the perfect *sari'* = M. *sari*, "I destroyed;"

pariḥ = M. *pari*, "I went." In Susian we find *naḥ* "I am" from the verb *en* "to be" with loss of the initial vowel.

The suffix of third person *ri* is often replaced by *ni* in Apirian, and this appears to be almost exclusively used in Susian.

Besides the three derivative tenses in *-ra*, *-da*, and *-ni* (the two first being often *ri* and *ti*), Apirian has a kind of correlative formed by the suffix *ba*.

The syntax is the same in the three dialects.

Examples of Susian.

naḥ Šutruk-Naḥḥunte šak Ḥalladuš anin šušinak gik sunkik anzan šušunḳa erizuib tibuḥi.

"I am Sutruk-Nahhunte, son of Halladus, the Susian king, powerful ruler of Anzan, I have united together the Susian warriors."

mašmi širmana šarraḥi, "here I placed the foundation."

Examples of the Apirian.

almūmaš Tirutur ḥu ulḥi dikra tibba šalḥuba išni XL *tartuk umi Napir ḥupakkir Dipti ḥuddanba ḥišmeš sirmuinni ardan.*

"Having gathered together the images of Tirutur, protector of this family (and) then having caused to be made there 40 (images) in all of the chiefs gods (and) of Dipti, I caused the enclosure for them to be established."

kimeš rukku Rappitum ukku Pirni šarara, šalzi undannamip ea. "I will place a great curse on these transgressors, unless they honour the house."

N.B.—The Medic and Apirian inscriptions are written by means of a few ideograms and a special syllabary, derived from later Babylonian soon after the fall of Nineveh, but Susian is written with characters hardly modified borrowed from old Babylonian.

OLD PERSIAN GRAMMAR.

PHONETIC.

The alphabet of old Persian differs from that used for the other languages of the cuneiform inscription. It has 24 letters:

The three vowels, *a*, *i*, and *u*.
The consonants are:—

Two aspirates, *h*, *ḥ*.
Two gutturals, *g*, *k*.
Two palatals, *c′*, *j*.
Four labials, *b*, *p*, *f*, *m*.
Five liquids, *n*, *l*, *v*, *r*, *y*.
Three sibilants, *s*, *š*, *z*.
Three dentals, *d*, *ṭ*, *t*.

The sounds of these letters are known to us only from the comparison of proper names and words found in the other languages, and are therefore to a certain extent uncertain. The letter *l* is especially doubtful, as it is only found in two proper names, and does not exist otherwise in Old Persian.

Those who studied first the Persian inscriptions have classified the letters in the following manner, and this order has been adopted in the glossaries which accompany their works:

	gutturals	palatals	dentals	labials	nasals	half-vowels	sibilants
Hard	*k*	*c′*	*t*	*p*	*n*	*y*	*s*
Aspirated	*ḥ*	—	*ṭ*	*f*	*m*	*r*, *l*	*š*
Soft	*g*	*j*	*d*	*b*	—	*v*	*z*

The simple aspirate *h* is left out and placed last.

If the classification of certain Indianists is followed we would have :—

	hard	asp.	soft	nas.	half-vow.	spirants
Gut.	*k*	*ḥ*	*g*	—	—	*h*
Pal.	*c'*	—	*j*	—	*r, l*	*š*
Dent.	*t*	*ṭ*	*d*	*n*	*y*	*s*
Lab.	*p*	*f*	*b*	*m*	*v*	*z*

Note. It must be remembered that the Old Persian is written by means of syllabic characters expressing one consonant and one vowel, the consonant being always first. This syllabary does not possess all the possible combinations, and such syllables as *ki*, *ḥi*, *c'i*, *cu'*, &c., could not be expressed; closed syllables, as *ak*, *ig*, *ar*, &c., could not either be written. It has been supposed that when we had such a group as *ka-i*, it was to be read *ki*, and that the final vowels are not to be read in many cases, *a-da-ma* being written for *adam*. The peculiarities of the syllabary may, however, be the result of the phonology of the language. It is more rational to suppose that if the writers of the Persian inscriptions had required the sounds *ki*, *ḥi*, *ak*, *ig*, &c., characters would have been invented for them, and it is more practical to take the language—the real pronunciation of which we cannot know for certain—such as it is given in the inscriptions. For the same reason have been rejected the *m̃* and *ñ*, which were supposed to exist by some scholars, though *never* written.

The vowel could be long or short. As initials they are always written simple when short or long; after a consonant the long vowel is expressed by repeating it after the syllabic sign: *māma* is written *ma-a-ma*, *dīša* is written *di-i-ša*, &c.

When the vowels are strengthened—or *gunated* as it is called by the Indian grammarians—*a* remains *a*, *i* becomes *ai*, and *u au*.

Final consonants of words or syllables are dropped: *paitā* for *paitar*, *napā* for *napat*, *kabaujīyā* for *kambaujīyā*. Two consonants are therefore never found together; the only exception is for the group *tra*, for which there is a special character.

There seems to have existed in Old Persian a kind of consonantal harmony, the letter changes are consequently very numerous; consonants influenced one another even over vowels and other consonants. The rules of these changes are very difficult to establish, on account of the small number of texts; and the exceptions to the rules which can be detected appear to have been numerous. A few of the changes are:

s becomes *h* after *a* and is often dropped altogether; it often reappears before *t* (see further on the forms of the verb "to be"); *s* becomes *š* after *i* and *u* (see the genitive formation).

t and *d* become *s* before *t*: *basata* past. part. from *bada*, before *c'* they become *š*: *avašac'aiya* for *avadac'aiya*.

k becomes *c'* before *t*: *c'aratanaiya* from the stem *kara*.

j becomes *ḥ* before *t*: *dūruḥatama* from the stem *dūrūja*.

All the consonants generally become aspirated before *r*, *m*, *n*, *š*, and *v*.

But as already stated there are numerous exceptions.

Formation of Words.

The great majority of the words are formed by means of suffixes. All words and stems end in a vowel, generally *a*; the suffixes can be superposed, that is, a word formed by a suffix may receive another to form a new word. The formative suffixes are:

(1.) *a* in *māragava*,[1] "a Margian," from *maragū*, "Margiana;" added to the *a* of the stem or of any word it gives us *ā*, which is the mark of the feminine, and is also found in some words: *dūvarā*, "door."

(2.) *at*, only in *napat*, "grandson," written *napā* in the texts.

(3.) *ana*, in *varakāna*, "Hyranian" (from *varaka*, "wolf").

(5.) *i*, in great many proper names: *faravaratai*, "Phraortes;" is a suffix of feminine names: *baumī*, "the earth;" *apai*, "water."

(6.) *iya*, in patronymics, names of populations and others:

[1] As proper names are not in the inscriptions preceded by any determinative we do not use capital letters.

haḣāmanaiŝaiya, "Achœmenid;" *bābairūvīya*, "Babylonian;" *marataiya*, "a man, *i.e.* a mortal."

(7.) *iŝa*, in *manaiŝa*, found in *haḣāmanaiŝa*, "Achæmenes."

(8.) *iŝata*, superlative formative suffix.

(9.) *u*, in *vahau*, found in the proper name *vahauka*; the *u* absorbs easily the other vowels, so this suffix may be the formative of *margū*, "Margiana."

(10.) *ina* forms adjectives of matter: *aṭagaina*, "of stone."

(11.) *ka* forms adjectives: *vazaraka*, "great, large."

(12.) *ta*, formative suffix of the past participle passive and old disused form of the ablative found in *parūvīyata*, and preserved as adverb formative suffix: *ṭakata*, "exactly."

(13.) *tama*, superlative formative suffix.

(14.) *tā* (for *tar*), in *paitā*, "father."

(15.) *tara*, comparative formative suffix.

(16.) *tarana*, in *dūvītātarana*.

(17.) *tā*, adverb formative suffix: *c'aitā*, "so long;" forms also other particles as conjunctions: *yatā*, "while."

(18.) *tāda*, with the final *a* assimilated in *ahaifaraŝatādīya*, locative, "in perdition."

(19.) *tana*, formative suffix of the infinitive, always found in the locative: *ṭasatanaiya*, "for speaking."

(20.) *tai*, in *ŝaiyatai*, "goodwill."

(21.) *tai*, in *ufaratai*, "Euphrates."

(22.) *ṭa*, same as *ta*, the old ablative, forms adverbs: *amūṭa*, "thence."

(23.) *ṭā*, perhaps same as *tā*, forms abstracts: *gaiṭā*, "possession," and also adverbs and particles: *avaṭā*, "there," *yaṭā*, "when."

(24.) *ṭai*, same as *tai*, in *dūvaraṭai*, "gate-way."

(25.) *ṭau*, same as *tau*, in *gāṭau*, "place."

(26.) *tra*, in *ḣaŝatra*, "empire;" *pautra*, "son."

(27.) *dā*, another form of the old ablative, forms adverbs and particles: *idā*, "here;" *yadā*, "when."

(28.) *na*, forms adjectives, as *asana*, "near;" and neuter nouns, as *satāna*, "place;" sometimes the inner vowels of the stems are strengthened: *daraujana*, "liar," from *dūrūja*, "to lie."

(29.) *nā*, in *faramanā*, "law."

(30.) *ma*, in *navama*, "ninth;" *darasama*, "strong, much."

(31.) *mā*, in *taumā*, "family."

(32.) *māna*, in *asamāna*, "heaven" or "sky."

(33.) *ya*, in *araiya*, "Aryan," perhaps same as *iya*.

(34.) *yau*, in *marašaiyauša* found in composition *uvāmarašaiyauša*, "self-killed."

(35.) *ra* forms adjectives and substantives of both genders: *zaura*, "violence;" *dūra*, "distant."

(36.) *vā* (for *van*), in *ḩašatrapāvā*, "satrap."

(37.) *vata* (for *vanta*), in *harauvataiša*, "the Arachorian."

This list might be extended, but the other suffixes, as well as some of the above, may have possibly the same derivation.

Particles, especially prepositions used as prefixes, form many words, not only verbs, but also nouns. The principal ones found in the texts are:

a or *ava*, augmentative in *amātā*, "trusted" (participle passive plural); *avahanama*, "dwelling-place."

a, privative in *anāmaka*, "nameless."

apa, "away," in *apagaudayāhaya*, "thou wilt hide away."

aparaiya, "according," in *aparaiyāyā*, "they conducted themselves according," *i.e.* "obeyed."

u, "well, good," in *ufarasata*, past participle, "having done well," before a vowel it becomes *uv*: *uvasapa*, "having good horses."

uda, "out," in *udaptatā*, "he arose."

upa, "over," in *upasatā*, "help."

nai, "down," in *naiyašatāyama*, "I ordered, imposed."

naija, "out," in *naijāyama*, "I went out."

parā, "away," in *parābara*, "he took away."

fara, "forwards," in *farābara*, "he gave, offered, presented."

hama, "with," in *hamataḩašaiya*, "I laboured," often abridged in *ha*: *hamātā*, "of same mother."

vī, "over," in *vīyatarayāma*, "we went over."

The formation of compound words is very free. These are, as in Sanskrit:

Copulative compounds, as in *garamapada*, name of a month.

Determinative compounds, as in *aradasatāna*, "high place."

Dependent compounds, as in *takabara*, "who wears a crown;" *asabara*, "one carried by a horse," *i.e.* "horseman."

Possessive compounds, as in *parūzana*, "having many branches;" *taḥamasapada*, "strong-hearted."

FORMS OF THE WORDS.

Nouns and Adjectives.

Nouns have seven cases formed by means of suffixes added to the nominal stem; for the singular we have:

(1.) Nominative formed by the suffix *ša*: *kūrū-ša*, "Cyrus;" *faravaratai-ša*, "Phraortes."

With the stems ending in *a*, the *š* of the suffix is dropped, the *a* of the stem is not always lengthened: *pāraša*, "a Persian;" *auramazadā*, "Ormazd."

With the stems ending primitively in a consonant, both consonants of the suffix and of the word are dropped, and the final vowel of the stem often lengthened: *paitā* (stem *paitar*), "father;" *napā* (stem *napat*), "grandson."

(2.) Vocative, in which the vowel of the stem is merely lengthened: *marataiyā*, "man!"

(3.) Genitive formed by the suffix *ša* added to the stem, the final vowel of which is strengthened: *kūrau-ša*, "of Cyrus."

The stems ending primitively in a consonant, retain this consonant followed by *a*, but the suffix is dropped: *paitra*, "of the father."

With the stems ending in *a* the genitive is formed in *ha* or *haya*: *auramazadāha*, "of Ormazd;" *ḥašāyaṭaiyahaya*, "of the king."

(4.) Accusative formed by the suffix *ma* added to the stem: *auramazadā-ma*, "Ormazd;" *bāǰī-ma*, "the tribute;" *bābairū-ma*, "Babylon."

(5.) Ablative. This case is formed by the suffix *ā*, but it is supposed that it primitively was *ata* or *ada*, which is still found as an adverb formative; it is confounded in form with the instrumental, and cannot be distinguished from it.

(6.) Instrumental, formed by the suffix *ā*: *kārā*, "with the army."

(7.) Locative. This case appears to be formed very irregularly: for the stem ending in *a*, we have *aiya* and *āyā*: *aramanaiyaiya* from *aramanaiya*, "Armenia," *arabairāyā* from *arabaira* "Arbela;" for the stems in *i* we have *yā*: *apaiyā* from *apai* "water;" for the stems in *u* we have *auva*: *babairauva*, from *babairū*, "Babylon."

For the plural the examples found are still fewer:

(1.) The nominative is, for the stems in *a*, *aha*, sometimes abridged in *ā*: *bagaha*, from *baga*, "god;" *ḥašāyaṭaiyā*, from *ḥašāyaṭaiya*, "king;" for the stems in *i*, it was probably *iya*, but there is no example; for the stems in *u* it is *va*: *dahayāva*, from *dahayāu*, "province."

(2.) The vocative is as the nominative.

(3.) The genitive is formed by the suffix *nāma*, rarely *āma*, added to the stem: *bagānāma*, "of the gods;" *dahayau-nāma*, "of the provinces."

(4.) The accusative is the same as the nominative.

(5.) The ablative is not found, but was probably the same as the instrumental.

(6.) The instrumental is formed by the suffix *ibaiša*: *bagaibaiša*, "by the gods;" *viṭa-ibaiša*, "by the tribes." With the stems in *i*, the initial *i* of the suffix is not repeated: *asabāraibaiša*, "with horsemen," from *asabārai*; it is rarely dropped after *a*: *rauc'a*, "day," makes *rauc'abaiša*.

(7.) The locative is formed by the suffix *šauvā* added to the stem: *dahayau-šauvā*, "in the provinces." With the stems in *a*, the *š* of the suffix is dropped: *anaiyāuva*, "in the others."

The feminine nouns have no special flexions, but take the same as the masculine. The neuter nouns are not distinguished either, the only peculiarity is that the nominative and the accusative are always similar: *ranc'a*, "day," nom. and acc.; *hamaranama*, "battle," nom. and acc.

This dual is found only in a few words, and especially those designing pairs as "ears," "hands," &c. The dual follows for the nominative and accusative the formation of the plural, but the locative is formed as in the singulār: *gauša*, "the two ears," nom. and acc.; *dasatayā*, "in the two hands."

Sometimes the same word appears to follow indifferently the formation of several classes; for instance, we find the accusative *baumīma* and *baumama*, the first being formed from the stem *baumī*, and the second from the stem *bauma*.

Some words have no singular, as *dūvarā*, "gate;" loc. *dūvarayā*, "at the gate," which is in the dual, a gate being considered as a pair composed of two pieces.

Adjectives are not distinguished by special flexions, but take the same as the noun; the genders are shown only by the formation of the stems, as in the nouns: for instance, in *vazaraka*, "great," the feminine is distinguished by the long final vowel of the stem: fem. *vazarakā*, gen. *vazarakāyā*.

The degrees of comparison are formed by means of suffixes, *tara* for the comparative, and *tama* for the superlative; the first is found in *apatara*, "the other," or "the more distant," and the second in *faratama*, "the first" or "foremost." Two other suffixes appear to have been in use by the side of the two first for the same purpose: *iyaša* for the comparative, and *išata* for the superlative; *iyaša* is preserved under the form of *yaza* (*š* having become *z*), in a proper name *vahayaza-dāta*, "better-gift," and *išata* in *maṭaišata*, "the uppermost." The words formed with these suffixes take the case-endings like the stems ending in *a*.

NUMERALS.

The cardinal numerals being always written in ciphers, their pronunciation is unknown.

Only a few of the ordinal numbers are known:

faratama, "the first."
dūvitaiya, "the second."
traitaiya, "the third."
navama, "the ninth."

From this last one it might be inferred that the ordinals were formed by the suffix *ma*.

We have also *aiva*, "the sole," or "the only," supposed to be derived from the word for "one."

PRONOUNS.

The personal pronouns are not completely known. We have: First person:

adama, "I," acc. *māma*, gen. *manā*.
vayama, "we," gen. *amāḥama*.

There are, besides the enclitic forms, *maiya* for the gen., and *ma* for the ablative of the singular; the acc. *māma* is also used as enclitic.

Second person:

tūvama, "thou" (really a vocative), acc. *ṭauvāma*. The enclitic form is for the genitive *taiya*, written once *taya*.

Third person:

The emphatic pronoun of the third person is expressed by the demonstratives; there are, however, special enclitic forms:

Sing. acc. *šaima*, "him," gen. *šaiya*.
Plur. acc. *šaiša*, "them," gen. *šāma*.

There are several demonstratives:

Hauva, "this one," found only in the nominative for the masc. and fem.

From *ava*, "that," we have neuter nom. and acc. *ava*, masc. acc. *avama*, gen. *avahayā*, plur. nom. and acc. masc. *avaiya*, fem. *avā*, neut. *avā*, gen. *avaišāma*.

From a stem *ima*, "this," we have: nom., masc. and fem. *iyama*, neut. *ima*; acc. masc. *imama*, fem. *imāma*, neut. *ima*;

gen. fem. *ahayāyā;* also written *ahaiyāyā;* inst. *anā;* plur. nom. and acc. masc. *imaiya,* fem. *imā,* neut. *imā.*

From the stem *ai* we have the neuter *aita,* "this."

Of the indefinite pronouns we have:

Nom. masc., *anaiya;* neut., *anaiya;* acc. masc., *anaiyama,* gen. *anaiyahayā,* abl. *anaiyanā;* plur. nom., and acc. masc. and fem. *anaiyā,* loc. *anaiyāuvā.*

The relative pronoun, which is better known, is:

	Masc.	Fem.	Neut.
Sing. Nom.	*haya,*	*hayā,*	*taya.* (Nom. and Acc.)
Acc.	*tayama,*	*tayāma,*	
Inst.	*tayanā,*		
Plur. Nom. and Acc.	*tayaiya,*	*tayā,*	*tayā.*
Gen.	*tayaišama.*		

The interrogative is *kā* for the masc., and probably for the fem. also, and *c'ai* for the neuter.

There is a demonstrative enclitic *dī,* which is at the acc. *dīma* in the sing., and *dīša* in the plural.

The neuter of the interrogative seems to have formed an enclitic, *c'aiya,* which is added to other pronouns to form new ones. It is to be noticed that before it the pronouns take their primitive forms: *anaiyaša-c'aiya* (for *anaiyada-c'aiya*), "something;" *avaša-c'aiya* (for *avada-c'aiya*), "whatever;" *kaša-c'aiya,* "somebody;" *c'aiša-c'aiya* (for *c'aida-c'aiya*), "something."

VERBS.

The classification and the system adopted in the Sanscrit grammar being equally applicable to the verbs of Old Persian, it is advisable to follow them as close as possible, as our texts are so few that many forms would be inexplicable, if we had not Sanscrit and Zend.

There are three persons, the first, the second, and the third, and two numbers, the singular and the plural; if the dual existed, no example has come down to us. The genders are not distinguished like they are in the Semitic verbs.

There are two different sets of personal suffixes for the active and the middle or intransitive voices. They are, as far as known to us from the texts—

Full forms:

	Sing.	Plur.	Sing.	Plur.
Act., 1st pers.	*mīya,*	*mahaya,*	Middle *aiya,*	*mahaya.*
2nd pers.	*haya,*	—	—	—
3rd pers.	*taiya,*	*taiya,*	*taiya,*	—

Short forms:

Act., 1st pers.	*ma,*	*mā,*	Middle *i,*	—
2nd pers.	(*ha*),	—	—	—
3rd pers.	*ša,*	*ša,*	*tā,*	*tā.*

R. The suffix of the 2nd pers. of the short forms often drops altogether.

R. With the verbal stem ending in *a*, the *š* of the 3rd pers. sing. and plur. becoming *h*, is dropped altogether and the termination is reduced to *a*.

Special endings are used to form the imperative:

Act., 2nd pers. sing.	*dīya;*	plur. *tā;*	middle sing.	*uvā.*
„ 3rd „ „	*tūva;*	„ —	„	*tāma.*

There are four tenses: present, imperfect, aorist, and pluperfect; and four moods: indicative, conjunctive, potential, and imperative.

The present is formed by adding to the stem the full forms of the personal suffixes: *dārayā-mīya*, "I hold," from *dāraya* (root *dara*).

The imperfect is formed by adding to the stem the short forms of the suffixes and prefixing to it the vowel *a*, which is called the augment: *abavama,* "I was," from *bava* (root *bau*).

When the verbal stem begins with a vowel, the augment forms

a diphthong with it or is elided. The augment is always placed before the verb, even if the verb is preceded by a preposition, forming with it a compound, and the augment is also in this case fused with the final vowel of the preposition: *avājanama*, "I was killing," from the preposition *ava*, and the stem *jana*.

These two tenses are called special tenses, because the stem of most verbs assumes a special form in them, and these special formations have been used as bases of the classification of the verbal stems by the Indian grammarians.

The aorist is formed by adding to the unmodified verbal root the short forms of the suffixes and prefixing the augment: *adā*, "he gave" (for *adāša*), from the root *dā*.

The pluperfect is formed by doubling the root of the verb, but as in Greek the consonant is weakened, *k* becomes *ć*; the only example known is the third person of the potential *ćaḥaraiyā*, from the very irregular verb *kara*, "to do."

The conjunctive mood is formed by adding *a* to the stem before the personal suffixes: *bavātaiya*, 3rd pers. of the present of the conjunctive, from *bava* (root *bau*). The characteristic *a* merely lengthens the final *a* of the stem.

The potential is formed by adding *ya* to the stem before the personal suffixes: *avājanaiyā*, 3rd pers. aorist from the compound verb *ava-jana*, "to kill."

As examples of the imperative we may quote: *pādīya* and *pātūva*, from the root *pā*, "to protect."

Besides these moods and the middle voice, the Old Persian verb had also two other forms—considered by the Indian grammarians as simple derivatives—the passive and causative.

The passive is formed by adding *ya* to the verbal stem, and takes the personal suffixes of the middle voice, from which it is distinguished only in the special tenses: *ṭahayāmahaya*, "we are called;" *asaraiyatā*, "he was broken," and several other examples taking the suffixes of the middle voice.

The causative, of which we have but few examples, is formed by adding *aya* to the stem, and it takes the personal suffixes of the active: *avāsatāyama*, "I caused to be placed," from *avasatā*, "to stand."

All verbs are supposed to be derived from a root, and they may be divided into ten classes according to the modification experienced by the root in the two special tenses.

(1.) The verbs of the first class are those the vowel of which is strengthened or lengthened, or as it is called in the Sanscrit, *gunated*, *a* of the root becomes *ā*, *i ai* or *ay*, *u au* or *av*, and takes the vowel of union *a;* the root *bau*, "to be," makes *bava* in *abava* 3rd. pers. sing. imperfect; *gūba*, "to speak," makes *gauba* in *gaubataiya* 3rd. per. present.

(2.) In the second class the root does not suffer any change, but takes directly the personal suffixes: *bara*, "to carry," makes *abarama* 1st pers. imperfect.

(3.) The verbs of the third class are those in which the first consonant is doubled: the root *dā*, "to give," makes *adadā* 3rd pers. imperfect.

(4.) In the fourth class the suffix *iya* is added to the root, the passive derivatives belong to this class: the root, *mara*, "to die," makes *maraiya* in *amaraiyatā* 3rd pers. imperfect.

(5.) The verbs of the fifth class add *nava* to the root: the root *vara*, "to declare," makes *varanava* in *varanavātaiya* 3rd pers. present of the potential.

(6.) The sixth class includes the verbs which take the personal suffixes with the vowel of union *a;* but as all words must end in a vowel in Old Persian, this class is practically the same as the second: *jīva*, "to live," makes *jīvahaya* 2nd pers. present.

(7.) The seventh class, which is composed in Sanscrit with the verb inserting a nasal before the last consonant of the root, practically does not exist in Old Persian, as a nasal at the end of a closed syllable is always dropped. The Sanścrit *band* is *bada*, "to bind," in Old Persian. See, however, further on, the form *akūnauša* from the root *kū*.

(8.) The verbs of the eighth class add *uva* to the root: *dana*, "to flow," makes *danauva* in *danauvataiya* 3rd pers. present.

(9.) In the ninth class the verbs add *na* to the root: *dī*, "to take away," makes *dīna* in *adīna* 3rd pers. imperfect.

(10.) The verbs of the tenth class add *aya* to the root, the vowel of the root is besides gunated: *gūda*, "to hide," makes *gaudaya* in *apa-gaudayāhaya* 2nd pers. present of the conjunctive.

The irregularities observed in certain verbs come from the fact that the same verb sometimes follows two or more classes in some of its forms, or that one verb is only used in certain tenses or persons, the others being supplied by another stem, as in our verb "to go," past "went." As a specimen, the verb "to be" might be given as far as it is known from the inscriptions: the root *as* in Sanscrit has become *aha*, but the *h* is generally dropped altogether, the primitive *s* reappears in the third person of the singular.

Perfect	sing.,	1st pers.	*amīya*,	plur.	*amahaya*.
	,,	2nd ,,	*ahaya*,	,,	— .
	,,	3rd ,,	*asataiya*,	,,	*hataiya*.
Imperfect	,,	1st ,,	*ahama*,	,,	—
	,,	2nd ,,	*aha*,	,,	*aha*
Conjunctive	sing.,	3rd. pers.	*ahataiya*,	,,	—

We have besides a third person plural with the suffix of the middle voice, *ahatā*, written once *ahata*.

From the root *bau* are taken the following forms:

Imperfect	1st pers.	*abavam*.
	2nd ,,	*abava*, plur. *abava*.
Conjunctive	3rd ,,	*bavātaiya*.

Potential aorist, 3rd pers. *baiyā*, with the change of *u* into *i*.

The verb *kara*, "to do," gives us another example. Most of its forms are taken from the root *kū*, according to the fifth class, *i.e.* with the suffix *nava* reduced sometimes to *na* (ninth class), or according to the second class. The forms found in the texts are:

Present conjunctive, 2nd pers. sing. *kunavāhaya*.
Imperfect, 1st pers. sing. *akūnavama*, plur. *akūma*.
Imperfect, 3rd pers. sing. *akūnauša* and *akūnaša*, plur. *akūnava*.

The form *akūnauša* must be brought back to the seventh class, with insertion of *na* in the root, the *n* not being dropped, because the stem ends in a double vowel.

Pluperfect potential, 3rd pers. *c'aḥaraiyā*, in which the *k* has become aspirated into *ḥ*.

Of the middle voice we have:

Imperfect, 3rd pers. *akūnavatā;* plural, *akūnavatā* and *akūtā*.

Of the passive derivation we have:

Imperfect, 3rd pers. sing. *akūnavayatā*.

The texts give us also the infinitive, *c'aratanaiya*, where the *k* is weakened into *c'*, and the past participle *karata* or *karatā*.

ADVERBS.

Nouns in the accusative, locative, and instrumental are used as adverbs; *nūrama*, "now," is no doubt the accusative of a disused noun.

The special formative of adverb was *tā* or *dā*, which is found in *ṭakatā*, "exactly, immediately;" *ada*, "then;" *idā*, "here," &c.

The negative is *naiya*. Another negative is *mā*, which forms, with the verbs, kinds of prohibitives. After this particle the augment of the verb is dropped: *mā tarasama* (for *mā atarasama*), "that I may not fear." Properly speaking this prohibitive particle may be considered as a conjunction.

CONJUNCTIONS.

The copula is expressed by *utā*, "and," and the two enclitics *vā* and *c'ā*.

The principal conjunctions are:

> *taya*, "that;" *ćaitā . . . yātā*, "till," or "as long . . . as;" *yadīya*, "when;" *mātaya*, "lest," &c.

Many of the adverbs are also used as conjunctions.

PREPOSITIONS.

The prepositions, which play, as we have seen, an important part in the formation of words, have a nominal origin, and are, when used isolated, found with the flexions: so we have *upā*, "on," instrumental of *upa*; the genitive *pataiša*, "to, against," and the locative *pataiya*, "for, at," from *patai*.

In the syntax will be given the list of the prepositions found in the texts, not in composition, with their meaning, their use, and the cases they govern. It need only be mentioned here that some prepositions are found only in composition, and that such a preposition as *pataiya* is used as postposition as well as preposition, and even as enclitic postposition, in which case it really forms a kind of flexion or case.

parā is used as a postposition with pronouns: *ava-parā*, "thereto," and with the flexion of the accusative, *hayā-parā*, "towards them," taken adverbially.

SYNTAX.

A noun in the singular may be used as a collective, taking the verb in the plural: *hayā amāḥama ḥašayaṭaiya aha*, "our (family) *were kings*."

In a few cases the same word designates the country and its

inhabitants: *pārasa*, "a Persian" and "Persia;" *māda*, "a Mede" and "Media." Sometimes a word is used indifferently in the singular or plural to designate a country: *mūdarāya* and *mūdarāyā*, "Egypt." The names of people are generally in the plural, *kūšaiyā*, "the Cossœans."

The dual is rare and generally replaced by the plural; it is preserved only to designate pairs: *gaušā*, "the two ears."

The force and meaning of the flexions had been to a great extent lost, and they are often replaced by prepositions.

The nominative marks the subject.

The genitive is used without preposition. The noun in the genitive may precede or follow its regent: *kūrauša pautra*, "son of Cyrus;" *vašanā auramazadāha*, "by the favour of Ormazd." The dative being lost in the nouns, it is expressed by the genitive: *kārahayā avaṭa aṭaha*, "he spoke so to the army."

The accusative marks the direct object, without preposition: *avama maṭaišatama akūnavatā*, "they made him leader." Without a preposition, or with the preposition *abaiya*, "to," it marks the direction towards a place, there can therefore be two accusatives: *avama adama farāišayama armīnama*, "I sent him to Armenia;" *abaiya avama nadītabairama ašaiyava*, "it went over to this Nidintabel." In this case, however, properly speaking, it marks the dative of direction.

The instrumental marks the manner: *vašanā*, "by the favour."

The ablative is never used without a preposition (see prepositions).

The locative is often used: *apaiyā*, "in water;" *nāvīyā*, "in boat;" *dahayaušauva*, "in the provinces."

The adjective agrees with the substantive it qualifies, in gender, number, and case: *ḥašāyaṭaiya ahayāyā bumīyā vazarakāyā*, "king of this great earth."

Often the adjective is united to the noun by the relative pronoun, which may be translated by the article: *kārama tayama hamītraiyama*, "the people the rebellious."

There is no agreement when the words are merely in apposition.

In a comparison the word compared to is placed after the comparative with the preposition *hac'ā*: *apatarama hac'a pārasā*, "other than Persia." After the superlative of comparison the genitive is used: *maṭaišatā bugānāma*, "the greatest of the gods."

The cardinal numerals are always written in ciphers, and are placed before the noun: XIX *hamarana*, "19 battles."

When the number is the total of a summation, it follows the noun: *faraharavama dahayāva* XXIII, "in all 23 provinces."

Cardinal numbers may be taken abstractly: VIII *ḥašāyaṭaiyā aha*, "8 were kings."

With the day giving the date the cardinal numbers are given, not the ordinal; the day is placed in the instrumental, preceded by the month in the genitive, and followed by the adverb "exactly:" *anāmakahaya māhaya* II *rauc'abaiša ṭakatā*, "on the 2nd day (lit. 2 days) of the month of Anamaka exactly."

The ordinals are real adjectives: *pataiya traitaiyama*, "the third time."

The personal pronouns are used emphatically with the verbs.

As there are no possessive pronouns, these are expressed by the genitive of the personal pronouns: *manā paitā*, "the father of me."

The enclitic pronouns are attached to nouns, pronouns, and particles, but not to verbs, except the enclitic *dī*, which is also attached to verbs. This union of enclitics is, after all, only a question of prosody; these words having no accent, were not considered as words in Old Persian, but written merely to the preceding word which happened to be before them. The enclitic has, therefore, not necessarily any connection with the word to which it is joined.

The relative pronoun agrees with the word it represents: *imā dahayāva tayā manā pataiyāiša*, "these provinces which pay homage to me."

The relative is used as a kind of article to unite words placed in apposition: *gaumātama tayama magūma*, "Gaumata the Magian" (accusative).

The distinction between the active and middle voices is

always made, though some of the forms of the two voices are confused. The middle and passive voices are much more often confounded. The middle voice is neuter or reflective: *hauva udapatatā*, "he rebelled;" *ḥašatrama hauva agarabāyatā*, "he seized (for himself) the empire." For the passive: *ava akunavayatā*, "this was done;" *hauva atrina basata anayatā abaiya māma*, "this Atrina was brought prisoner to me," these two examples will be sufficient.

The pronoun subject of the verb is often expressed even when the noun is already given. In the last example, for instance, it is really: "he, Atrina, was," &c.

The present requires no explanation.

The imperfect answers exactly to the English past: it is the historical tense. It expresses also, like the imperfect of the Latin tongues, a lasting action prolonged sometimes even till the present: *adama-šaima avājanama*, "I killed him;" *avahayā kabaujīyahayā barātā aha*, "a brother was to this Kambysés;" *adama-šāma ḥašāyaṭaiya aham*, "I was (and still am) their king;" *kāra haya nadītabairahayā taigarāma adāraya*, "the army of Nidintabel was holding the Tigris."

The imperfect has sometimes, especially after *yaṭa*, the force of pluperfect: "I worked;" *yaṭa gaumāta vīṭama tayāma amāḥama naiya parābara*, "so that Gaumata might not have superseded our clan."

The aorist answers to the past perfect, and expresses an action quite finished: *haya imāma baumīma adā*, "who has given this earth." The aorist also may have the force of a pluperfect: *kāra hac'ā yadāyā faratarata, hauva hacā-ma hamītraiya abava*, "the army had separated itself from duty, it became rebel against me."

The conjunctive mood is used to express the future: *adataiya azadā bavātaiya*, "then knowledge will be to thee."

The potential expresses a doubt or a wish, and is used for conditional: *auramazadā-taya jātā utā-taiya taumā mā baiyā*, "may Ormazd be thy enemy and no family be to thee."

The imperative expresses an order or a wish. Often a sentence begins in the potential and finishes in the imperative:

utā-taiyi taumā vasaiya baiyā utā daragama jīva, "and may a numerous family be to thee and live long."

The infinitive, always in the locative, is used as in our modern tongues after another verb, but without any preposition: *aiša hadā kārā pataiša māma hamaranama c'aratanaiya,* "he came to do battle against me with an army."

The negative is generally placed before the verb: *haya manā naiya gaubataiya,* "who does not call himself mine." It is also placed before noun: *adama naiya baradīya amīya,* "I am not Bardes." And it is repeated before every noun and even adjective: *naiya aha marataiya naiya pārasa naiya amāhama taumāyā,* "there was no man, neither Persian, nor of our family."

The conjunction *taya* unites simply two phrases; the verb of the second may be in the indicative: *taya adam amīya,* "that I am."

After *yaṭā* the imperfect is used when it means "when," and the conjunctive when it means "in order that." *Yadīya* governs the conjunctive in the conditional sentences. When it means "when" it is followed by the imperfect.

The prepositions found in the texts are:

abaiya, "to, against," with the accusative.
abaiša, "on," with the locative.
anūva, "along, on," with the locative.
atara, "in," with the accusative.
ayasatā, "with," with the accusative.
upā, "for," with the accusative.
uparaiya, "over," with the accusative (in two doubtful passages only).

pataiya alone, or with the ordinal number in the neuter, it is used for "again" or "time:" *pataiya traitaiyama,* "the third time;" in these cases it may be a neuter noun, used alone or with an adjective as adverbial locution. With nouns this particle is postposed, with the instrumental "in, by:" *vītā-pataiya,* "in clan," with the locative "on:" *uzamayā-pataiya,* "on a cross."

pataiša, "against," with the accusative.
paraiya, "on, about," with the accusative.
pasā, "behind," with the genitive.
hadā, "with, by means of," with the instrumental.
hac'ā, "by, from," with the ablative.

Syntax of Sentences.

Old Persian is rather free in its construction. As a rule the subject stands first and the verb is thrown to the end of the sentence, immediately before the verb is placed the complement, and before this one the object; the indirect object precedes the direct object: the formula is therefore s-i-o-c-v. The determinative of time, place, or state is generally placed at the head of the sentence before the subject: *pasāva kāra bābairūvīya hac'ā-ma hamītraiya abava*, "then the Babylonian people became rebel to me."

When there is an emphatic statement, the verb is placed first: *tātaiya dārayavauša ḥašāyaṭaiya*, "the king Darius said;" *naiya aha marataiya*, "there was not a man."

The reason of the action follows generally the verb; the indirect object, being confounded sometimes with it, is also thrown back after the verb in some cases: *pasāva hamītraiya hagamatā paraitā pataiša dādarašaima hamaranama c'aratanaiya*, "then the enemies gathered together (and) came to make battle against Dadarses;" *hamītraiya abava hacā-mā*, "they became rebel against me."

The complement and the object may be also placed after the verb: *vašanā auramazadāha kāra haya manā avama kārama tayama hamītraiyama aja vasaiya*, "by the favour of Ormazd my army killed the rebel army in great number;" *adama kārama faraišayama bābairūma*, "I sent an army to Babylon."

When the subject is expressed emphatically it is sometimes placed near the verb after the object: *babairūma hauva agarabāyata*, "he took Babylon for himself."

The mention of a date is a determinative, and placed at the beginning of the sentence: *atraiyadīyahaya māhayā* XVII. *rauc'abaiša ṭakatā aha*, "it was exactly on the 10th (lit. the 10 days) of the month of Atriyadiya."

When the verb has two objects one is often placed after it: *adam hadā kamanaibaiša marataiyaibaiša arama magūm arājanama utā tayai-šaiya faratamā marataiyā anūšiyā ahatā*, "I with faithful men killed this Magian and his chief followers who were with him."

The complex period offers no difficulty, as every one of its members is considered as a compound expression, and placed in the same order as the simple elements of an ordinary sentence.

The sentences beginning by "if, when," &c., are considered as determinative and placed before the principal sentence: *yātā adama bābairūva ahama imā dahayāva tayā hac'ā-mā hamītraiyā abava pārasa uvaja*, &c., "when I was at Babylon, these provinces, which became rebel against me, (were) Persia, Susiana," &c.

The following sentences will show that the construction is very regular:

naiya aha marataiya naiya pārasa naiya māda naiya amāḥama taumāyā kašac'aiya haya avama gaumātama tayama magūma ḥašatrama dītama c'aḥaraiyā, "there was not a man, neither Persian, nor Medic, nor any of our family whoever, who could have taken the power from Gaumata the Magian."

We have in this last sentence an example of double accusatives: *ḥašatrama dītama* is really the complement of the verb: literally it is "who could have made Gaumata, the power taken away."

kārama vasaiya arajanaiya haya paranama baradīyama adānā avahayarādīya kārama arajanaiyā mātaya-māma hašanāsātaiya taya adama naiya baradīya amiya haya kūrauša pautra, "he killed many people who had known the old Smerdis, for which reason did he kill the people: 'lest they should know me that I am not Smerdis who (is) the son of Cyrus.'"

kašac'aiya naiya adarašanauša c'aišac'aiya ṭasatanaiya paraiya gaumātama tayama magūma yātā adama arasama pasāva adama auramazadāma pataiyāvahaiya, auramazadāmaiya upasatāma abara, "any one dared not say anything about Gaumata the Magian till I came, afterwards I prayed to Ormazd, Ormazd brought me help."

pasāva hauva kāra haya manā kapada namā dahayāuša mādaiya avada māma c'aitā amānaya yatā arasama mādama, "afterwards this army which (is) mine waited for me there, a province of Media called Kampada, till I reached Media."

THE END.

PRINTED BY BALLANTYNE, HANSON AND CO.
EDINBURGH AND LONDON.

LaVergne, TN USA
05 August 2010
192259LV00004B/104/P

9 781143 709869